COME WITH ME
TO ST HELENA

B W Marshall

MINERVA PRESS
LONDON
MIAMI DELHI SYDNEY

COME WITH ME TO ST HELENA
Copyright © B W Marshall 2000

All Rights Reserved

No part of this book may be reproduced in any form,
by photocopying or by any electronic or mechanical means,
including information storage or retrieval systems,
without permission in writing from both the copyright
owner and the publisher of this book.

ISBN 0 75411 158 X

First Published 2000 by
MINERVA PRESS
315–317 Regent Street
London W1R 7YB

Printed in Great Britain for Minerva Press

COME WITH ME
TO ST HELENA

Introduction

This book is a day-by-day relation of the events experienced by the author in going on a holiday to the remote island of St Helena in the south Atlantic Ocean from the moment of boarding the Royal Mail Ship St Helena at Cardiff docks on 2 January, 1994 to finally disembarking back in Cardiff on 6 May, 1994.

For anyone interested in small remote islands and their ways of life, this work really is a must.

The RMS, as the ship is affectionately called, is the only constant link with the United Kingdom and South Africa, the island being its principal reason for existing.

I hope that as you read these pages, you will be able to visualise yourself as the actual traveller.

The voyage distance out, via Tenerife, was 4,340 miles and the return via Banjul and Tenerife was 4,375 miles, an overall total of 8,715 miles. Quite a journey.

2 January

Arrived at the embarkation room for RMS *St Helena* at Cardiff docks before 2 p.m. as requested. Actually aboard the ship at 3.20 p.m.

We stood in dock until 8 p.m. and were out of the docks and lock system by about 9.15 p.m.

First meal aboard, at 8 p.m., was attended by every passenger. This was preceded by life-jacket drill in the sun lounge at 6.30 p.m.

What a night this was... We left the bar at a few minutes after midnight, but by 1 a.m. the seas had become really rough and in no time at all loose fittings and furniture were being hurled here, there and everywhere.

There was a horse on board en route for Tenerife. I don't think this weather could have done him any good. The chief purser did warn us that this storm was imminent at the life-jacket drill session as his colleagues had had advance warning from the weathermen.

Just after 1 a.m. the engines cut out and the whole ship was plunged into darkness, but this was rectified quite quickly. It turned out that we had not been too far away from Lundy Island whilst this was happening. All other shipping had been refused permission to leave harbour during this storm. One of our stabilisers had come out of the water and also the anchor had swung free and had crashed into the side of the forecastle, creating a largish hole.

With a total of 1,519 nautical miles from Cardiff to Tenerife, and no interim ports of call, all this was a little worrying. It eventually transpired that the ship had been over at an angle of thirty-six degrees at one point.

3 January

There is a force nine gale blowing, causing a large majority of the passengers to be confined to their cabins with sea sickness. This was coupled with the dangers associated with falling over or being thrown around, due to the exaggerated lurchings of the ship.

At breakfast I saw only twelve of the one hundred plus passengers, and at lunch time only about twenty.

At this point we were averaging 13.7 knots per hour.

By midday we had travelled a total of 183 nautical miles, leaving another 1,336 to go to Tenerife. Our position was latitude 49°20', north, longitude 6°16' west with a south-westerly wind and an air temperature of 7°C/45°F; sea temperature 11°C/52°F.

A ship's company boat drill was performed at 4.30 p.m.

The storm continued throughout the night, registering thirteen on the Beaufort scale at one point. The waves were well above the porthole level on the third level deck and the creakings of the inside cabin walls left one with a feeling of trepidation.

4 January

Daylight arrived with the gale reading at force eleven.

At midmorning (9 a.m.) came an announcement over the tannoy system by the captain.

'We are about to move to one side and run with the wind, giving us an opportunity to study the damage to the forecastle. Please stay exactly where you are and either sit down or preferably lie down.'

This caused some consternation among the passengers, but in actual fact the manoeuvre passed by almost without notice.

At midday our position was latitude 45°15' north, longitude 09°13' west and we had covered 293 nautical miles during the last twenty-four hours, leaving another 1,064 to Tenerife. Our average speed for this period had fallen to 11.4 knots due to the atrocious weather conditions, making our overall rate of knots since leaving Cardiff 12.19 per hour.

The air temperature was up to 11°C and the sea temperature 13°C, the wind was now west-south-west at force eight.

It will be noticed that the total distance covered and the distance left to the next port, do not necessarily match exactly. This is due to weather conditions, causing some slight movement from a true course.

It will also be noticed that sea and air temperatures are now rising well – as should be expected. Even the sun is shining now.

We were invited to attend the captain's cocktail party at 6 p.m., in the main lounge, but due to still poorish weather and the number of passengers still confined to their cabins, this was postponed for twenty-four hours.

Saw a film in the sun lounge during the evening. A comparatively quiet night, making a welcome change.

5 January

Even more rough seas this morning!

One can feel the temperature slowly climbing but the weather is still not very good. Our midday record was latitude 40°10' north, longitude 10°20' west. Distance travelled over last twenty-four hours, 319 nautical miles, giving a total travelled of 775 nautical miles. Our average speed for twenty-four hours was 13.3 knots, giving an overall average speed of 12.6 knots. We have 745 nautical miles left to Tenerife.

The air temperature is 14°C/57°F, sea temperature is 15°C/59°F.

There is a preponderance of rain and sea mist from 2.30 p.m. The captain's cocktail party is again postponed because of the weather, but who cares? One can get 'legless' with the ship rolling like this without having a drink.

The total steaming time to date has been 61.4 hours. For those mathematically minded, this is where the 12.6 knots total average speed comes from.

At one point during the early evening, a sudden lurch by the ship caused every chair – occupied or not – and table in the sun lounge to go hurtling into the far corner, right alongside the bar. That caused a few choice comments, especially amongst those who eventually finished up alongside their chairs.

6 January

Woke up with the ship still tumbling about roughly in heavy seas.

At 11.40 a.m. dolphins were seen on the starboard side and at 5.20 p.m. the first seagulls appeared.

At midday our position was put at latitude 35°16' north, longitude 13°48' west, having travelled 317 nautical miles during the last twenty-four hours. The nearest land to us now was the beautiful island of Porto Santo near Madeira.

We have 427 nautical miles to travel to arrive in Tenerife.

Our average speed for this leg was 13.2 knots per hour, giving an average to date of 12.79 knots. The wind was north-westerly at force seven and is forecast to drop to force six or even five. The air temperature is 13.6°C/57°F, sea temperature 16.8°C/62°F.

There was nice warm sunshine from about 2 p.m. and seats were put out on the sun deck for the very first time this voyage. Some quite sickly looking passengers, whom we had not set eyes on since the first night, appeared.

I went up to the bridge in the afternoon (and every afternoon afterwards).

The captain's cocktail party eventually took place at 6 p.m.

Spent the evening in the sun lounge drinking away to the last of the bad weather.

The worst of the storm was undoubtedly over; we had been through what I am told is probably the worst weather any of the ship's crew had ever known – and we are still here. In the knowledge that it will never get worse, then there is no real reason why anyone should not take this voyage. It was most definitely quite a dramatic episode.

For those who were interested, keep fit classes were held in the sun lounge from hereon every afternoon for the remainder of the voyage.

7 January

Up and on the sun deck in lovely early morning sunshine at 8 a.m. This was much more like it. A fresh breeze to dry out the freshly scrubbed deck, and only three other passengers up to enjoy it with me. This is what I call tranquillity.

A school of dolphins off the starboard side crossed ahead and beneath the ship and at 11.50 a.m. Nolan saw a turtle.

Quite hot all day today.

At midday our position was latitude 35°16' north, longitude 29°20' west and we had covered another 370 nautical miles at 15.42 knots per hour, leaving only 53 to go to Tenerife where we disembarked at 4.30 p.m. Our average speed to date has been 13.36 knots, air temperature 18°C/65°F, sea temperature 20°C/68°F.

We spent about seven hours ashore and sailed out of Tenerife just after midnight.

The time spent in harbour had been spent by the ship's crew members welding the hole in the forecastle.

Whilst on shore we went to three different bars and found that three pints of beer were variously priced at 900 pesetas, 1,500 pesetas and 600 pesetas – all for exactly the same product. It does tend to prove how wary the holidaymaker needs to be on Tenerife.

Bed about 1.40 a.m. after a convivial evening in the sun lounge (we do not seem to spend much time in the main lounge at all). Anecdotes were topical and the one about a spilled dinner and lost false teeth during the storm by an elderly lady named Phyllis deserves to go down in local folklore.

Taking on fresh water, restocking with fresh fruit and refuelling were all performed at Tenerife.

8 January

Up and about at 7.45 a.m. but very leaden skies – I didn't quite expect that. Still on the dullish side at midday.

Distance from Tenerife to St Helena will be 2,821 nautical miles. Incidentally, for those who wonder, there are 1,760 yards to one land mile but 1,820 yards to one nautical mile.

Played cards to while away these dullish hours.

During the afternoon we enjoyed good sunshine, but it was accompanied by a strong sea breeze.

We seem to be spending all of our time in company of the 'Saints'. One couldn't ask for better.

Our midday position was latitude 25°31' north, longitude 16°46' west. We had travelled 179 nautical miles since leaving Tenerife and had 2,642 to reach our target of St Helena.

In 11.5 hours of steaming we had averaged 15.6 knots per hour. And our nearest point of land was just south of Agadir in Morocco. The air temperature was 18°C/65°F, sea temperature 20°C/68°F with the wind north-north-west at force four.

9 January

Brilliant hot sunshine today. This is what it is all about. Plenty of sea birds about from 10 a.m. to after noon at which point we were off the coast near the border of Mauritania with Senegal.

We were at latitude 19°36' north, longitude 17°49' west. Over the twenty-four hours to midday we had covered 360 nautical miles at 15 knots per hour, leaving 2,281 nautical miles to go. Both air and sea temperature were recorded at 21°C/70°F.

The last of the sea birds had disappeared by 2 p.m. and a slight and pleasant sea breeze appeared at about 3 p.m. Lots of dolphins were around the ship just after 4.15 p.m. and also three sea turtles and two humpback whales.

At 9 a.m. four of us were taken on a tour of the engine room etc.; it was most interesting. All of the ship's crew are of the same attitude and cannot do enough for us. One bar steward by the name of David Williams has promised to take Nolan sea fishing in his boat when he returns from Cape Town in March.

We spent the evening – until 2.30 a.m. – drinking and talking and generally enjoying ourselves in good company. Nolan came out with, 'I think I'm getting drunk, granddad!'

10 January

Up and on deck at 7.50 a.m. to view the coastline and islands off Dakar, Senegal. It appears to have been largely given over to the French tourist trade, as a sort of Riviera. The view was a little misty, probably due to the early hour, but still quite reasonable. Sunshine was mixing in as the sun was rising quite steeply and sharply. It is nothing like I'd imagined it to be – there seems to have been quite a lot of cash invested here. Dakar is one of the largest and most proficient ports on the whole West African coast.

An island stands at the entrance – variously used as a slave collection point and later as a prison.

Some small motor-powered canoe-type fishing boats seen up to five miles off the coast. That looks a decidedly risky occupation to me.

By 8.30 a.m. the sun was now fully out. Another hot day was beginning. A boat drill was performed at 10.30 a.m.

Played quoits on the funnel deck, and we partook of a barbecue on the sun deck at 8 p.m. This was a resounding success. The size of a piece of beef, cooked for upwards of one hundred and twenty people is quite staggering.

At midday our position was latitude 13°45' north, longitude 17°26' west and we had travelled a further 356 nautical miles at an average speed of 14.8 knots per hour. We had 1,925 nautical miles still to travel and our air and sea temperatures were both 21°C/70°F.

This was another late night in this company – 3.15 a.m. this time. The sea was like a millpond.

11 January

Didn't realise it was so hot and humid, but on going on deck at 8 a.m. it was just like Singapore. It was like this all day long.

We saw plenty of flying fishes throughout the day, and twice a couple of humpback whales – probably the same two each time.

A clay pigeon shooting competition during the afternoon, followed in the sun lounge by a film and then a visit to the crew's quarters where they put on a disco for us until well after 2 a.m.

The day's steaming details at midday: latitude 08°08' north, longitude 16°11' west. Day's distance travelled 352 nautical miles at an average speed of 14.67 knots per hour, 1,573 nautical miles left to go. The air temperature was 27°C/81°F and the sea temperature was 28°C/82°F.

12 January

Ship rolling a little bit from 7 a.m. to 9 a.m.

Humid again.

At 10 a.m. the temperatures were recorded as air 30°C/86°F; sea 29°C/84°F.

However, at midday they read air 26°C/79°F; sea 29°C/84°F. We were now off the coast of Liberia, and our position was latitude 02°54' north, longitude 13°50' west, having travelled 344 nautical miles, leaving 1,229 to go. Our average speed for the twenty-four hours was 14.33 knots per hour. Wind south-east and force three.

A humpback whale seen blowing off to starboard, about one mile away, at 1 p.m. Still lots of flying fish around us.

Played quoits on funnel deck in afternoon and skittles on sun deck in evening.

Saw a film about Ascension Island at 5 p.m.

In the afternoon it was very hot but with a good sea breeze relieving the humidity.

We are due to cross the equator just after midnight.

13 January

Crossed the equator at 1.30 a.m.

Laundry returned today – done really well and beautifully pressed and ironed, along with dry cleaning. The ship does have facilities for those who wish to do their own washing and cleaning, which I understand are very good, but I like being made a fuss of.

Sun was shining very strongly at 8.15 a.m. The sun deck is well rigged out for the 'crossing-the-line' ceremony, even down to both the blue and red ensigns being displayed. The actual 'ceremony' is probably the highlight of all the organised activities on the ship – absolutely brilliant. Nolan, along with two others, received his certificate as a 'shell back' making him an 'official citizen of the denizens of the deep'. It is quite impressive. As this occurs on the RMS *St Helena* every couple of months, the captain and crew have got the whole event to a fine art.

So many flying fish were in evidence that it was impossible to judge within a couple of hundred just how many I saw.

Games were held in the early evening that were designed to encompass all age groups and a whist drive was held in the sun lounge in the later evening for those who so wished.

Earliest night in bed for over a week – 1 a.m.

The steaming details for the twenty-four hours to midday were: latitude 02°19' south, longitude 11°37' west; 340 miles sailed at an average speed of 14.17 knots per hour, 888 nautical miles still to be travelled.

The nearest land was Gabon.

14 January

On deck at 7.30 a.m. Sun well up and hot, but a good breeze keeping things very pleasant. The sea was most placid.

Virtually two weeks at sea now and virtually no boredom whatsoever is showing – except possibly a couple of islanders returning home who 'can't wait much longer' because of either emotional or other quite rational strings.

It is surprising how many more people there now are on deck taking the sea air at this early hour today. There are not many left lying in their bunks.

Even the usual percentage of toffee-nosed travellers are becoming almost approachable – except for some east coast Canadians whose voices are incessantly booming in the background. It takes all sorts to make a world.

At 8 p.m. the air temperature was 28°C/82°F, although at midday it was 25°C/77°F and the sea temperature 27°C/81°F.

The nearest land was Ascension Island, with our position reading latitude 07°37' south, longitude 09°24' west, having steamed 345 nautical miles. Only 543 left to go.

Our rate of knots was 14.37, giving an overall average of 14.64 knots per hour since leaving Tenerife 155.5 hours earlier. The wind was reading south-east at force four.

During the evening a fancy dress or hat parade was held, with every contestant receiving a bottle of bubbly for their efforts.

Got to bed at 3.30 a.m.

There were still a number of flying fish around during the daytime but at night-time, sadly, a couple of fishing vessels and the mother ship – all Japanese – appeared lit up out of the darkness between St Helena and Ascension Island, with trawl nets dragging up to twelve kilometres behind them, catching everything, from the smallest of fish right up to dolphins.

15 January

A lovely morning. Up and on deck at 7.15 a.m.

This was the last full day of this outward voyage. Had a very interesting little chat with a lady about what used to happen, probably forty years ago, when the schoolchildren on St Helena used to catch and kill rats and then cut off their tails and sell them to government officials for either a penny or two pence each, as part of the rat extermination project. It is now a fact that virtually no brown rats are left on the island. A comforting thought.

There are not quite as many people on the sun deck as there were yesterday morning, probably due to most of them trying to get a good night's sleep in prior to the early risings required tomorrow, as the ship is due at the anchorage at Jamestown at about 6 a.m.

Light cloud cover moving across us at 8.30 a.m., coupled with a fresh breeze. The ship is beginning to pitch and toss a little.

The midday readings were: latitude 12°40' south, longitude 07°11' west; 330 miles steamed, 213 left to go. Average speed 13.75 knots per hour, giving an average of 14.52 since leaving Tenerife.

Air temperature 24°C/75°F and sea temperature 25°C/77°F, wind south-east at force four.

Man overboard drill was performed at 4.30 p.m. and was most impressive from an onlooker's point of view.

A film was shown in the sun lounge during the evening at 9.15 p.m., following which, with five 'Saints', Nolan and I stayed up all night in the main lounge waiting and watching for the first appearance of St Helena. It was well worth it.

16 January

Arrival

The island became clearly visible at 5 a.m., and by 6 a.m. workmen had arrived by barge and boat to carry out their duties.

We paid our £6 each landing fee then we didn't bother with breakfast, but instead transferred to the launch, and then on to the landing steps, at 8.30 a.m.

Then a hiccup... We had to wait for over two hours for our cases to be brought ashore.

We arrived in Blue Hill village at about 11.30 a.m. The smell of cooking greeted us, and whereas we had fully expected to do our own cooking and washing, we found that Florrie was prepared to do it all for us. She did us proud at dinnertime with a large serving plate of chicken portions and pieces of pork – about eighteen in all – with lots of baked and roast potatoes and fresh cabbage.

There was, in reality, enough for several meals.

Her family called round during the evening and we spent a really pleasant evening.

I turned in just before 10 p.m. to try and catch up on all of my lost sleep. The fact that we had called in at the Oasis in Half Tree Hollow during the early afternoon had just about seen me off, especially as the sun had been so very hot.

17 January

The Island

This morning I was originally woken up by a very heavy rainstorm at about 6 a.m. which came and went for the rest of the day. I found it very soothing to listen to on the corrugated roof. Actually got up at about 8 a.m.

Had 'plow' for the first time today. It's good. Set off at 3 p.m. with Gavin and Nolan and did a tour of quite a lot of the island, taking in a visit to Hutt's Gate Store to deliver a parcel for Mrs Johnson.

The roads are narrow – averaging about eight feet – and hilly, and to an outsider must be very dangerous. The rule that applies here, over and above all others, is that a vehicle travelling downhill has to give way to one travelling uphill. Everyone follows this rule.

We went to Dot's Café in the Market Hall and then, after a brief tour of the shops in Jamestown, went to the White Horse public house for an hour or so. Very pleasant. Then back, via Jacob's Ladder and the Barracks, through Half Tree Hollow and home to Blue Hill.

Saw my first wire-bird running – not flying – along the road, and also a hen pheasant. There are plenty of rabbits about, and also a field full of donkeys. In addition to these, there are also plenty of domestic cattle, pigs, sheep, and goats.

18 January

A nice fresh morning.

Quite a flock of fairy terns wheeling around in the valley below us. The prevalent noise in the background is of mynah birds calling, along with domestic fowl. By 8.30 a.m. High Hill is basking in sunshine and in the distance the ocean is glittering as the sun's rays catch it through the break in the hills of the valley.

There are lots of Swainson's canaries flittering around and also quite a number of little barred ground doves. Later on, about 9 a.m., some malagasy fody appeared. They are little beauties, and are locally called red-birds or cardinals. Talking of local names for birds, it appears that any bird with a red breast is called a robin. By now the whole valley is pleasantly cosseted in gentle sunlight and a lovely cool breeze is blowing through the trees and banana plants.

There are numerous pathways through the forest in the Blue Hill area, so today we tried some out. At 10 a.m. we set off along by a side path which joined the road at Blue Hill Store, and then left it again to go around the back of High Hill and down to close by the ocean. At this point, we turned around and made our way back.

There were lots of lovely plants around, especially everlasting flowers (yellow helichrysum), blue weeds, wild bilberry (Cape gooseberry) and wattle. Of this last plant, we saw a man collecting a large sackful of seed pods. They are similar in appearance to sweet-pea pods, but are on a tree or bush.

After a rest of about two hours we set off again around High Hill, this time through the valley at the foot of it. This is really a very pleasant stroll with not too much climbing involved, and here we saw agapanthus, liquorice bush, self-seeding dahlias, fuchsias and monkey toes. Also there were domestic goats and a very peculiar sheep with black wool on the body and a long white tail. It looked very odd.

19 January

It rained a little during the night, and now, early in the morning, everything smells fresh and vibrant. On the veranda is a cricket about one and a half inches long with a black head and a brownish-tan body, and in the garden several ladybirds, marked a little differently to those we are accustomed to seeing in the UK, but nevertheless unmistakable. Also there were a few inevitable snails brought out of hiding by the rain.

The largish black and white common mynah birds are now calling in unison quite aggressively with whistles and screeches down in the valley below, backed by a chorus from the pockets of domestic fowl in isolated homesteads scattered in the forest around, and calls from the ground doves. The whole valley and surrounding countryside is now wide awake. Gavin and Florrie have brought in some lovely mackerel; a dozen or more. I had one for my breakfast.

The fairy terns are wheeling round again – I suppose that we will be getting these every day from now on. They are known locally as the 'white birds' and other than a large black eye patch, are totally white, except when they are chicks, at which stage they are grey. Being sea birds they do, of course, have webbed feet. They are extremely graceful in flight.

Looking at the red cardinals flitting around amongst the aloe trees, they appear to be quite destructive of flowering shrubs as they search for insects. Both the cardinals and the canaries appear to favour the loquat trees. The fruit on these trees grows in abundance.

About 9.30 a.m. a team of workers – together with a tractor – appeared in the valley forest and began sawing down the dead trees. Quite a job on these hillsides and narrow pathways.

There is quite a proliferation of gorse (furze) around, very pretty in flower with the bright yellow standing out quite clearly, but I am told that it is proving very difficult to eradicate from the pasture land. It was originally introduced to the island as a fuel plant, and is still occasionally used by some cottage dwellers for this purpose.

The principal pasture grass is kikuyu grass, and it sends out long stolons, so wiping out most of its competition. Although only brought to St Helena in 1934, it is very well established, to the detriment of the various 'hay' grasses.

Clouds from the sea caused slight mist and rain about 11 a.m., making crickets shout in unison, but this soon passed over.

In the afternoon we went for a drive to the picnic area at Horse Pasture. This is well and thoughtfully equipped with a nice play area for children, and also barbecues built along the wall for those who want to use them. It is quite a large area, liberally scattered with bushes, and frequented by wire-birds, canaries and Java sparrows – flocks of them. It is a really nice place. Later went to Thompson's Wood and collected a bag full of purple granadillas (passion fruit); there is a small glade full of them.

20 January

Nolan and Gavin went sea fishing just after 3 a.m. with three others in a catamaran. Went out about fifteen miles and between them caught two barracudas, two tuna (one a monster, they tell me), old wives, bull's eyes and deep water mackerel. Obviously they thoroughly enjoyed themselves.

I spent the day catching up with my writing. Not very exciting I know, but it had to be done, and it was quite a dull day weather-wise anyway.

For supper we had fried bull's eye. Lovely.

In the late evening, under a clear half-moon, we walked around the general area of Blue Hill village. On returning and switching on the electric lights, we drew quite a gathering of moths and a couple of ordinary houseflies. They even exist here, as do some very small but annoying mosquitoes. This genus do not carry the malaria virus, but still give an unwelcome bite.

21 January

At about 10 a.m., we went into Jamestown and looked around the shops. One thing to be done was to cash an ordinary English bank cheque. At Soloman's bank it is possible to cash traveller's cheques, but not ordinary ones. But at the government offices in the castle grounds there was no problem whatsoever, all that was required was one's passport for means of identification and then the making out of the cheque to 'The St Helena Government'.

After this, there was a visit to Dot's Café for a cup of tea and then to the White Horse pub for a beer. I also called on the Chief Education Officer at the Canister in Main Street and we arranged for a pen pal and school link-up with island children and the children of Hardwick primary school in Banbury.

On the journey out of the heat of Jamestown, we saw the lovely thorn trees – also called kaffir booms – sporting really beautiful red flowers. There are lots of these trees near Knollcombes, and it is from the nuts or seeds of these that local craft beadwork is produced. These trees are used all over the island to mark various boundaries as their thorns make them resistant to cattle and goats and other grazing animals, although these animals do appreciate the foliage.

The next trees of real note were the Cape yews, which have been introduced, as the name indicates, from South Africa. They produce some very fine timber. Also scuttling around them I could hear the calling of chukar partridges, although I must confess I did not see any of these very secretive birds and the same thing has to be said of the ring-necked pheasant which, I am told, is seen only infrequently and hides in woodland.

Another very noisy little bird is the waxbill or avadavat. This is St Helena's smallest bird – a tiny brown and greyish finch – and has a most distinctive chirrup. Although possibly the most sombre bird on the island in appearance, when looked at closely, it is seen to be tinged with pink on its underparts and also has a coral beak and has a longish black tail. Not so sombre after all.

22 January

It rained for most of the morning, so I spent the time looking through the records of famous or well-known men who had been to visit the island over the years. For those interested, these names include Juan De Nova Castella, commodore of the Portuguese fleet returning form India in 1502; the first inhabitant of St Helena Dom Fernando Loper in 1516; Captain John Dutton, who in January 1659 was commissioned by the English East India company to colonise St Helena under the terms of its charter from Richard Cromwell, Lord Protector of England, Scotland and Ireland. He was requested to 'settle, fortify and plant' and was appointed governor-in-chief.

For the record, he sailed with four hundred men and arrived on 5 May, 1659. Within one month, a fort was erected and named Castle of St John – later James Fort. Just inland from this defensive position, settlers houses were erected up the valley, which became known as James Valley. The name James was chosen as King James II was at that time the monarch.

The Dutch did make a successful landing on New Year's day, 1673, in an attempt to wrest the control of the island from the English for their own use, but on 5 May of the same year, the British re-took it with a naval bombardment of Jamestown and a landing of three hundred and fifty men on rocks in Prosperous Bay, now known as Keigwin's Point, after the lieutenant in charge of the operation.

Two men, a slave known as Black Oliver, and a soldier named Tom, made this landing possible. Oliver was the guide and Tom performed a superb feat of climbing to get a rope down for his comrades. As the men swarmed up they shouted, 'Holdfast, Tom!', and ever since that day, the cliff has been known by that name. It turned out that these heroics were unnecessary as by the time the men reached Jamestown, the Dutch had already capitulated to the naval bombardment.

In 1676, the twenty year old astronomer Edmund Halley – of comet fame – visited St Helena, and he did so again in 1699 when commanding the expedition ship HMS Paramour. In 1739 Robert Jenkins – of the War of Jenkins Ear – became the governor for a period of two years. Captain Cook visited when voyaging home from his second circumnavigation of the world in May, 1775, and Captain Bligh of the Bounty called in 1792. The year 1836 saw the arrival of Charles Darwin in HMS Beagle. His *A Naturalist's Voyage Round the World* is still housed in the castle at Jamestown. It was presented by Darwin to commemorate his visit. In 1890, the Zulu chief Dinizulu was a prisoner on the island and remained as such for seven years. HRH the Prince of Wales visited in August, 1924, and in 1947 Queen Elizabeth II – then Princess Elizabeth – visited with her parents in HMS Vanguard on the royal tour as did Prince Andrew in 1984. One other man not to be overlooked is Captain Joshua Slocum, the first lone circumnavigator of the world, who called in 1898.

In the afternoon the sun won through and it became very well up in the eighties. Went into Jamestown which was buzzing with life. The RMS was in from Ascension Island, and had brought the eagerly awaited mail.

23 January

Out early this morning recording bird song. This is the time for it with mynah birds, finches, waxwings, partridges, cardinals and canaries all vying with each other to outshout the domestic cockerels.

The night was very windy, but by 9 a.m. it had eased off and everything was very peaceful. There was just a little movement among the upper branches of the eucalyptus trees in the valley, and in the aloes and wattle, but the maritime pine and Monterey cypress are made of sterner stuff and were showing no movement at all.

With a local boy, Leroy, as a guide, we went along 'The Ridge' and across Ebony Plain down to Thompson's Bay. This is quite a walk and care is needed on the high hillsides with a sheer drop down to your left as you go seawards. We disturbed a number of feral pigeons in the cliffs and also saw a pheasant in amongst the pine needles that have built up over the years. On the ridge itself, we saw three very large donkeys that were wild. I am led to understand that if you can catch one, the forestry and agriculture people will pay you for it. There were also a fair number of wild coffee bushes there and they were all in flower. It really is a beautiful spot. The whole of the afternoon was sunny and very hot.

24 January

It rained solidly from about midnight until about 10.30 a.m., just what the people living in the countryside hereabouts require for their small and well-stocked gardens. The soils here are moderately acidic and a local source of calcareous sand can be used in place of imported lime at a much cheaper price. The potassium content of the soils is high and the phosphorus is quite adequate, although there is some deficiency of nitrogen. A particular chilli bush stands in a garden in Blue Hill that must be four feet high and as much around, and is heavy with chilli pods. As this plant is quite hard to grow – the world over – then the soil here must be good. Plants that occupy quite a large portion of these gardens tend to be sweet potatoes, pumpkin vines and a various assortment of European vegetables. Yams – bencoolen or bangalore – are prized for their delicious flavour, although three other yams are also cultivated in and around these garden plots. Geraniums, begonias, canna lilies, barberton daisies and agapanthus – my favourite – grow in profusion. I can only try to convey the beauty of the island's countryside. An individual has to see it for himself to fully appreciate it.

There are at least seven types of banana growing on the island, some wild and some cultivated. The more usual ones are coast bananas, madeiras and finger bananas, and there are also plum trees, loquats, pawpaws, peaches, pears and purple granadillas (passion fruit). This latter some of the islanders consider to be an aphrodisiac. Cape gooseberry, known as bilberry, and both wild and cultivated guavas, grow in quantities between one and two thousand feet up, along with buddleia, Bougainvillaea, bamboo, plumbago and periwinkle, and several kinds of hibiscus and the lovely-named sweet-scented ladies' petticoats (called moon flowers locally), together with masses of wild fuchsias.

The rain had fetched out about a dozen or more garden snails in one particular garden, but a dusting with cooking salt killed off these destructive pests.

By 11.30 a.m. the sun was shining – it is surprising how quickly the weather can change here. In the space of one hour we have gone from torrential rain to bright hot sunshine.

Went to Jamestown in the evening to celebrate Nolan's birthday. The people are absolutely unbelievable. They have only known us for just over a week, yet we are treated with open arms. Where else in the world will we be able to find this?

25 January

We had a wet morning again, but it cleared up by 9 a.m. and the sun was shining. With all this early morning rain, it brings to mind a saying attributed to a Boer prisoner of war back in 1902. He referred to the climate of the island in the comment, 'There are two seasons, one the rainy season, in which rain is the rule and sunshine the exception, and two, the dry season, which resembles the rainy one so much that the mistaking of one for the other has never yet been ascribed to ignorance'.

About 11 a.m., we set off towards the columns of Lot and Lot's Wife, but did not get too far as the clouds came down and obscured the view somewhat, so we turned around and moved back down into the sunshine. Wild bilberries were growing in profusion here, as were European blackberries, and in the distance on some rocks were a couple of goats that I took to be wild ones. A few do manage to exist on the more inaccessible cliffs, and there are quite a number of these cliffs as it is estimated that about sixty per cent of the island is what is referred to as 'eroded waste'. Well, that it may be, but it is certainly very spectacular. As a matter of fact, environmental degradation is now being reversed under the guidance of Kew Gardens in a suitable environmental and development strategy.

Quite a few of the endemic plants need some help. The she-cabbage, the large St Helena rosemary and St Helena salad plant (longwood samphire) are quickly brought to mind of these trees and plants, although it is almost certainly too late for the boxwood.

On the other side of the coin, the St Helena scrubwood, another endemic plant, is now recolonising naturally, and a tree that was considered to be already extinct, the ebony, is now becoming re-established thanks to careful propagation by the forestry authorities. This tree was almost extinct in 1771 according to contemporary accounts, and was assumed totally extinct in about 1850. It was rediscovered in November, 1980 when two examples were found clinging to a cliff edge in the region of Blue Point. Seedlings are nurtured at Scotland and then transplanted to suitable cleared land on Ebony Plain. This area was originally covered with prickly pear plants prior to the land being given over to the ebonies.

26 January

This proved to be quite a day as we went to Scotland, Rosemary Plain, High Point, back to Rosemary, Sandy Bay – but not quite the whole way – and then via High Peak back to Blue Hill. Scotland itself is very important for the useful work done by the Agriculture and Forestry Department as well as being a very lovely spot. There were numerous birds around, but one I had not expected to see was a moorhen. I just cannot imagine how this breed of bird first arrived on St Helena. I have been glibly told that they took the place of rails. That still does not explain how.

At High Point, we saw plenty of morning glory flowers growing along the roadside, alongside clumps of wild nasturtiums and a few irises. This is a place of immense beauty overlooking Lemon Valley, and it has a hairpin bend that defies description. Back up to Rosemary and we called into a two-storey house, quite unusual in the countryside, in order to purchase garden produce from the owner. He sold us peaches, onions and cucumbers and also gave us parsley and dates. Also on his premises he produced figs, loquats, mandarin oranges, plums, pears, apples, and such flowers as African marigolds and strelitzia (bird of paradise). There is no way to fully describe the beauty of this island.

The next visit was the side road down to Sandy Bay, alongside the many banana plants growing wild and the marvellous sweet-scented ladies' petticoats, creamy white trumpets hanging limply in amongst the clumps of wild fuchsias. A little way on and we came to the coffee grove, very well cultivated and adding its own touch of beauty to the place as well as some very welcome revenue. There was also wild ginger there.

At the Baptist chapel at Sandy Bay, we decided not to continue on down the hill, but to leave it for another day and double back along the lane to rejoin the road near High Peak. This was becoming enshrouded with clouds by that time. We passed the now totally invisible Lot and Lot's Wife columns, and returned to base at Blue Hill.

Most evenings the clouds roll in over the hills, but rarely get down into the valleys very much. It all adds to the magic of the place. There is, of course, plenty of rain in the valleys at evening time and during the night and morning, leaving the whole setting at over a thousand feet high looking very verdant. It is from the sea level to one thousand feet that the arid zone predominates, and that has its own type of beauty.

27 January

Went into Jamestown this morning and decided to enter it by leaving the Barracks at the top of Jacob's Ladder and descending the steps into the town. One needs to know about the Ladder to appreciate this feat; it is undoubtedly the most spectacular feature of the town. It is 699 steps in height, or 602 feet, and 933 feet long. In other words, for every three feet you travel you drop a further two. Originally built of wood in 1832 by the military – a Lieutenant GW Melliss supervised – and rebuilt in 1871 – as part of a system for hauling articles up and down by means of a capstan bar and ropes, assisted by mules. Only the steps now remain. One would think that coming down would be easy but don't believe it; it is not. The islanders tell me it is equally leg-trying both ways and I believe them. I have not tried going up yet, but coming down after about five hundred steps the balance seems to go a little, and on arriving at the bottom it is hard to get the knees to co-operate properly.

What an experience that was. We spent the next two hours in the consulate recovering.

Near by is the Canister, and outside it stand two very old peepul trees with twisted trunks. They reminded me of just how my knees felt at that moment.

28 January

Lovely sunshine from quite early this morning. Plenty of bees and butterflies amongst the flowers and the beans in the gardens, and the crickets calling incessantly.

Decided on a day in Jamestown which – when we got there – was decidedly hotter. In the town area itself, there were plenty of mynah birds and pigeons which are all virtually finger tame, and some of the flowers and trees growing in the town limits are really pleasant. In upper Jamestown is a blue flowering jacaranda tree that is a joy to behold. These trees occur throughout the island, but this particular one is a real beauty. There is a large Bougainvillaea that totally dominates the castle gateway, and there are superb ficus trees in the public gardens. Other blue jacarandas occur around the area known as the Grand Parade. The whole area is colourful and vibrant.

I have read in one book the words, 'The green belt of trees, shrubs and gardens relieve the monotonous vista of corrugated roofs'. Well, the greenness of everything, I agree, is pleasing but I do not agree there is any monotony. There is something to interest one every few yards if looked for. The whole town is one of life and happiness with no place for monotony. My only complaint is that all the hills are not downhill.

We spent some time in four of the five licensed establishments in town during the evening. That was very pleasant as well. For those wanting it, there is a disco held at Sandy Bay every Friday evening. Nolan went with friends to it, but not me. I prefer the old-fashioned pubs, and anyway, my muscles were still playing up after the Jacob's Ladder excursion yesterday.

29 January

Another day filled with sunshine and bird song. I went into the woods to record some as I find this very satisfying, and the canaries especially are very obliging.

Around 11 a.m. we went up High Hill again in order to find an alternative route to the summit, but although we did find the best alternative, we decided to turn back when almost there as it appeared a touch of foolhardiness would be involved.

During the hot afternoon we went past the Head O'Wain medical clinic that serves the local community and on to Saddle, which is a smallholding-cum-farm shop that does a fair business. Most European vegetables are grown and sold here, and the tomatoes especially are real beauties.

There are many Java sparrows and canaries here in flocks. One thing that we saw on the way back that we had not reckoned with was a swarm of bees across the roadway. Fortunately we did not upset them in any way.

In the evening we went into Jamestown and the noise of the countless numbers of mynah birds all shouting at once was absolutely incredible, with the main column of noise emanating from the general locality of the trees opposite the Market Hall. Immediately outside the Market Hall – seemingly in opposition to the mynahs – the Salvation Army were in full voice, and with all the shops in town remaining open until 9 p.m. on Saturday, there was certainly plenty of life around.

The market hall is a Victorian wrought-iron building which was refurbished and reopened in 1990 and is definitely a building of character – and characters.

30 January

This was a day with a difference. Although the whole of it was very, very hot – in the nineties – I spent it indoors talking to Ernest Roberts, an eighty-seven year old from Plantation who, having originated from Blue Hill, had spent some years in both England and Ascension Island, but had, nevertheless, spent most of his life working on St Helena. He had visited Cape Town and spent three spells of two years on Ascension and he had also served a while in the army in the UK. Most of his working life had been spent working at the saw mills of Plantation stables to which he had to journey five miles to and fro on foot from Horse Ridge daily as there was no transport available in those days. Often it was a case of going to work in the dark and returning home in the dark and it needs to be borne in mind that there is virtually no level ground at all on the island. He also kept me enthralled with his fishing exploits, especially of his – and his friends' – use of ropes in getting to the best fishing rocks. This man is quite a character with a mind that has all of the alertness of a young man, and he has done enough travelling outside St Helena to be able to make sound judgements. He loves his island home.

Whilst talking to him I was brought a spray of lovely red flowers of the eucalyptus tree and he immediately went into a conversation on the various merits of the uses of the wood of this tree. Before I knew it, he was then describing the loading of guano into boats on Ascension Island. As I say, the alertness of his mind is amazing.

It was only the oncoming darkness and the incessant chirping of the crickets that brought the conversation to a close.

31 January

Another warm day but with a slight breeze during the morning. I went on another walk early on recording bird song, and when I returned about 10.45 a.m., I found both Florrie and Nolan out in the part of the garden area most in danger of being taken over by kikuyu grass attempting to put the matter right. At least one little short-nosed field mouse had the fright of his life whilst this was going on. One area that they uncovered revealed at least forty pineapple plants as well as something that I had not noticed before – a clump of wild sunflowers. They differ from the European ones in that the centres are yellow, not black.

About midday we set off to a point overlooking Sandy Bay and over to our left we could clearly see High Peak with its crown of Norfolk Island pine trees looking majestically over the whole coastline of the island – well, about 345° to be more precise, as a bit of it is out of view behind Diana's Peak. To our right was Thompson's Hill and we knew full well that the vines that carry the passion fruit were there growing on and near the loquat trees, so we made for the spot. We were a little too early because apart from one ripe one, all the others that we could find were still green. However, there were now lots of ripe blackberries to be had for the taking.

On rejoining the road it is possible to see Speery Island which, I am told, is covered in guano but is the best place to view trophy birds between it and Man and Horse pastures.

Coming back towards Blue Hill village, we now realised that the eucalyptus trees had all come into wondrous flower virtually overnight. If you have ever seen these flowers you know what I mean, but if you haven't, then you don't know what you have missed. They are lovely. As we re-passed the point overlooking Sandy Bay, we stopped and gazed out over it. The sky was clear of all clouds and everything was as clear as crystal. The crater area is almost like looking at the moon. It is definitely recommended viewing. Lot and Lot's Wife are in the foreground from this position and, along with the Asses' Ears, are phonolite intrusions, as indeed is High Hill. In fact High Hill, overlooking Blue Hill village, is the largest phonolite intrusion on the whole island.

On arriving back in the village we were shown some badly damaged sweet potatoes which had been attacked – would you believe it – not by slugs or snails, but by pheasants. Oh yes, we were also presented with a lovely handful of honeysuckle for the house. It really is surprising just what does grow here.

We did see an absolute giant of a cockroach late in the evening, but other than being a nuisance to householders they do not have any poisonous tendencies and are controlled anyway by the Public Health Department by spraying. There are only a few of these and they occur only in the dry barren zone. There were once St Helena earwigs but these are believed to be now extinct and have been since the 1960s.

1 February

The gardening session yesterday seems to be paying dividends already, as the pumpkin have come into flower overnight. When these things happen here, they happen fast.

Having seen that cockroach yesterday, I asked if there are snakes on the island, but there are none. That's nice to know. There is just one gecko. It is very shy and colourless and only a few inches in size. When noticed it is usually on window panes or walls. It is harmless.

During the morning we took a pleasant walk, first along the tarmac road and then up an earth track to the area known as barren ground and it was here that I first noticed the real difference between the black and green wattle trees. It is a fact that the slower you walk, the more you see – or at least the more you take in.

During the afternoon we went first to Rosemary – to the house we had visited six days earlier – to purchase potatoes and runner beans that were grown there, and whilst there noticed that other than the flowers already mentioned there were also dahlias, agapanthus and geraniums growing in secluded spots. From there we moved on to Scotland and its lovely blue jacaranda trees; then Hutt's Gate and Longwood before going on to the Woody Ridge mill, once a flax mill, but now given over to agriculture and visited by pheasants as I saw them for myself, then Levelwood and the Silver Hill Bar, which is a very picturesque area, then on to Rock Rose – the entrance is marked by a very large Norfolk Island pine that is believed to be well over two hundred years old and is the largest on St Helena. (If it were not for the New Zealand flax lining the road hereabouts, I think that perhaps a touch of vertigo would show its head.)

This portion of the journey, before we reached Green Hill, appears to be the wildest of the lot as regards the flax, which seems to dominate all else.

Green Hill is a vista that is spellbinding. A nice picnic spot has been made there looking across to Diana's Peak in one direction and Sandy Bay in another, linked by High Peak and good pastureland. Some of the cottagers around these areas live in splendid isolation and appear to be among the most easy-going people on earth. Always a smile and a wave, even to people they have never met before. From Green Hill we moved on to the ridge around Sandy Bay – where we noticed that the wild banana trees were carrying quite a lot of fruit – and so back via High Peak, from which spot it was easy to see that the sea was looking angry, back to Blue Hill.

The angriness of the sea become apparent at about 9 p.m. when a heavy storm broke. It continued throughout the night.

2 February

It was still raining until 9.15 a.m. – over twelve continuous hours of it – just what the island gardeners wanted.

Confined to barracks, as it were, by the weather, I decided to find out about the geology of the island. It is between forty-seven and forty-eight square miles in size and is obviously of ancient volcanic origin, being largely of basalt and associated extrusive rocks. The highest point is Mount Actaeon at 2,685 feet, followed closely by Diana's Peak. Flagstaff Hill is 2,257 feet and the Barn is 2,021 feet. From a central point of the island, the various ridges lead outwards to the east and west and are tilted steeply to the south before being broken by the coast at Sandy Bay.

There are very steep-sided valleys reaching right down to the coast between huge domes and humpbacked masses. The most obvious are the broad-topped ones as at the urban sprawl at Half Tree Hollow, and the tapering ones as at Friar's Ridge which drops over the cliff tops at Lemon Valley Bay. Some of the rock is quite treacherous, especially on the north-east part at the Barn and Flagstaff Hill.

The areas most clearly recognisable as having been the centres of ancient volcanic activity are the spectacular vistas of Sandy Bay – and the Gates of Chaos, how well named – and the area around Knotty Ridge. One by-product of this activity is the old Cornelian mine on the opposite side of Turk's Cap valley. Cornelian is a form of silica and is semi-precious. It is formed by heating dykes by lava flows.

At both Sandy Bay and Knotty Ridge it appears that lava flows have come from a number of fissures, rather than from the central vent as is usual for volcanoes, and consequently high basalt domes have resulted.

The whole island is a little more than three miles at its widest point, and its drop of 1,620 feet at Great Stone Top is its sharpest precipice. Near Great Stone Top is the Bell Stone. It is what remains of a phonolitic column that earned it its name. It would ring like a bell when struck. I'm told it does not do this as well as it used to before it was damaged.

By 2 p.m. it was again raining heavily, which it continued to do continuously until dusk, but we were fortunate inasmuch as the local island charabanc called in at Blue Hill school with a party of – would you believe – Christmas party revellers from the post office. They called on us to join in with them and we had a lovely friendly afternoon. A nice picnic and drinks of both alcoholic and ordinary types were thrown in. As I've said before, their friendliness is absolutely genuine and unforgettable on this island.

3 February

The morning began with a visit to St Paul's church, a lovely and well-kept building in Whitegate. When we arrived there at about 9.30 a.m. the bishop was outside ringing the bell for a church service. If ever there was a haven of peace and tranquillity then this is it. We signed the visitor's book and had a look around and believe it was time well spent.

St Paul's church was opened in 1851 and is now the cathedral, but it does have commemorative plates on the walls over one hundred years older. It was build to replace an earlier seventeenth-century church, and was chosen by the inhabitants as the seat of the bishop, so becoming St Paul's Cathedral in 1859.

From here we went on into Jamestown, past the hospital and up Constitution Road – and what a climb that is – before turning sharp left into Field Road. As we looked back down into the town way below we could see numerous prickly pear and mango plants, as well as cotton plants, growing on the hillsides all the way up. The view of Jamestown and the harbour was a magnificent sight well worth keeping in the memory as well as photographing.

Coming around the hill to descend into Rupert's valley is not something to be tackled by anyone liable to suffer from vertigo. This side of the valley is far steeper than Ladder Hill. As you come down past the government-owned Power House, you find on the left hand side a whole row of coconut trees that were planted in the mid-1980s and a pleasant oasis of garden flowers that are beautifully tended on the right side of the road. Behind the coconuts stands the St Helena canning factory which deals with tuna, etc. The road eventually ceases for motor transport on the Fisherman's Wharf.

Turning round and returning to Jamestown we called in to the public library which has a surprising number of books of the island locked behind a glass-fronted case in the reference section. One book I looked at, *The Definitive St Helena* (JC Mellis, 1875) I would suggest to anyone as obligatory reading if interested in natural history. He actually produced a list of 907 different plants. Some were so rare that I will give you two examples:

Wild mango – only one plant. It is at the Briars.
Sumach plant – only one plant. It is in Plantation Gardens.

There are many such references.

The whole day turned out to be very hot, especially down in the town, so after a cup of tea in Dot's Café and a visit to the handicraft shop – which is well worth a visit – we returned to Blue Hill. It's cooler up there.

4 February

At 9.15 a.m. we went to Willowdene where the people who lived there were collecting strawberries for afternoon tea – and picked up two companions to join us in a walk around Diana's Peaks. We then moved on and collected three more at Black Gate and, at 9.45 a.m., the seven of us set off up the hillsides.

There are fantastic views from here looking across at Flagstaff, The Barn, Sugar Loaf, Great Stone Top and Little Stone Top. As we entered the flax country it became very obvious that several springs rise in this area, and the pathway, already well overgrown with the flax, becomes very muddy. Care has to be taken. What we did see were several he-cabbage and black cabbage trees as well as five grass frogs which, even in this area, are considered to be quite rare. Also we saw – and handled – several blushing snails.

Actually on the highest point of Diana's Peak, we found a box containing a rubber stamp and pad which reads... 'Stamp, and bring down the former one'. This we did. I hope the 'Dingle Clan' have received theirs by the time we get back to England. We sat and had a cold drink before descending through the clouds that were threatening us, but fortunately they then left us.

The journey was undoubtedly hard work down via the non-too-clearly-defined pathway – if that's the word – but to be honest, it was quite enjoyable. Coming out clear of the flax just above Black Gate, we sat down among the cowpats and thoroughly enjoyed our hard-earned picnic. It was then a case of walking down to the tarmac road and going on to Silver Hill Bar where we called in and partook of life-saving beverages.

The clouds moved in and away so swiftly at the peak area that we saw the whole island and then virtually nothing several times whilst we were up there. During the evening we were given some nice refreshing rain that everyone seemed to enjoy, even a visiting lizard.

One moment memorable above all others on this walk was when, having squished through the flax and marshy thicket I decided to stand for a moment, regaining my breath and trying to commit the vision to memory, knowing I might never return to this lovely spot. It is an easy spot to fall in love with.

5 February

The others went fishing this morning but I chose not to. Instead, I took a walk in the nearby woods and valleys. For anyone wishing to really get to know St Helena, it is necessary to spend a lot more time here than I am doing at the moment but it is essential not to waste a moment, if it can be avoided. Apart from learning the geography of the island, one must find out about the effect of sunshine and of rain, and the 'Saints' themselves and their ways of living and working and playing. I really believe we are making friendships that will last as long as we do. These people do sometimes set off to walk to their destinations on the tarmac roads in the knowledge that if any car or lorry passes them travelling in their direction, it is more than likely to stop and offer them a lift.

I did notice at one point that an attempt has been made to stop the process of erosion by the apparent digging of a trench in a gully and firstly aloes had been planted there and later Port Jackson willow. Sensible and very practical. Having mentioned this, I've since been told that this has been done in several places.

Moving on farther, I came within a very short distance of High Peak. There are black and he-cabbage trees (but not she-cabbage trees), whitewood, dogwood, St Helena lobelia, large and small bellflowers and of course the impressive tree ferns. It is a very impressive part of the countryside. High Peak is often covered in mist or cloud which can envelop it in minutes. As this was happening now, I retraced my steps into the valley, but the rain did eventually catch up with me. However, within twenty minutes or so I was again dry, thanks to the hot sunshine that followed. With such an ebb and flow of rain and sun the gardens are looking very strong and healthy and the birds and bees and butterflies are flittering in and out of the buds and flowers doing their bit. I think that the garden of Eden was based on St Helena.

About 4 p.m. the 'fishermen' returned with a fair-sized conger eel and several jacks and greenfish, having been fishing from the rocks down in Sandy Bay. They had barbecued one between them whilst they carried on with their fishing. The greenfish were used as bait. A catfish was used in the same way.

During the evening we visited Jamestown which was bristling with life as it always is on a Saturday evening with the shops being open until 9 p.m. This is a ploy that undoubtedly acts as a magnet for the islanders – and visitors for that matter. There is a mobile fish and chip shop that pulls in at the top of Market Street that produces food equal to any I have ever tasted from this type of outlet. One thing I did not expect to find on St Helena was a fish and chip shop, although there are a couple of cafés that produce good meals as well.

6 February

Heavy rain at night, followed by a strong drying wind and then bright sunshine. The die was cast for a successful day early in the morning. At 10 a.m., I noticed that a lot more lilies have come into flower down in the valley, and that for some reason all the birds seem to be even more vociferous than usual.

We had planned a walk with friends along the area referred to as Hooper's Ridge during the afternoon, but this plan has to be cancelled as, at about 1.45 p.m., the clouds moved in and the rain simply poured down. When it rains like that you don't move far. By the time the sun took over again, it was too late to go, but in no time at all we were surrounded by flower-spangled meadows, all outrageously beautiful because of the rains. With the background of canaries, cardinals and fairy terns, there can be few sights better than this.

At about 4 p.m. we went to Head O'Wain and then on to Barren Ground where we found a small copse full of vines bearing purple granadillas. Many were ripe, so we picked and ate those, leaving many green ones to be returned to in about a week's time.

The evening saw us back in Jamestown where we called in at the Standard public house and saw on the wall there – amongst other things – a large framed commemorative of Oxford United's appearance in the 1986 milk cup final. That was most unexpected, 4,700 miles away.

I had brought a twig of a plant back from the walk to Diana's Peak to get identification. I had the answer to the problem this evening. It was a cinchona. The bark of cinchona is used to make quinine and was originally grown here deliberately in the late 1860s. It was not an economic success but, as I'd just proved, it is still eking out an existence in the wild. Apparently quite a number of these plants can be found on Mount Actaeon, as they like the environment.

7 February

It was so very hot today that a gentle stroll in the general vicinity was sufficient effort to make during the morning. It was during this idle walk that a stray thought crossed my mind. The Miss World competition every year does not ever include a girl from St Helena. These girls are probably excluded because, with one of them in it, it would be no contest. I have yet to see one that was not pretty, to say the least.

Near the High Hill we found a small stand of about two hundred young pine trees planted in straight rows in a patch surrounded by older pine trees, obviously put here to counter any threatened erosion. The Agriculture and Forestry Department can be clearly seen to be doing a good job throughout the island.

On arriving back at the house, we found grasshoppers in the garden. We had seen crickets here before, but not grasshoppers. There are also plenty of caterpillars in the garden on the dahlia and agapanthus leaves. As the afternoon wore on, it got even hotter so I decided to simply sit back and enjoy it and listen to the birdsong in the valley below.

About 6 p.m., the others went fishing again, this time to Rupert's Bay. I went to the stile leading to High Peak, but again came back without attempting to climb it. It was a lovely evening for a walk and I managed more than a dozen photographs of the area, hoping to catch several moods of the weather as the clouds came and went. The mountains seemed to change from dull grey and brown to orange and mauve as the light changed from dark to sunny and back again. Down by the stile I noticed some of the largest clover leaves I have ever seen. I suppose that that is because of all the moisture from the clouds. On the way back I passed a man with his car boot up, and he was cutting grass and flax at the roadside with a scythe. I jokingly asked him if he was enjoying himself and he entered into a conversation with me in which he told me he was cutting food for his animals. A very practical attitude to life.

The fishing party got in just after 4 a.m. They had certainly had a night on the rocks. As far as I can tell, the only fish they caught this time were soldiers, six in all and hardly worth the effort. But they had enjoyed themselves. They said they had hooked larger fish – but those were the ones that got away.

8 February

The partridges were calling well this morning. They've been on the island for over four centuries now as they were referred to by Captain Thomas Cavendish of HMS Desire way back in 1588. Of other birds on the island that dates can be put to, the mynah bird was introduced in 1885 by a Miss Phoebe Moss, who released five at the Briars. These birds are now almost at pest level. In 1852 thrushes, larks, starlings and blackbirds were introduced, and from Indonesia Java sparrows in the early 1800s. The common waxbill, from South Africa, was introduced at the same time. The wire-bird is the only bird that is a true native of St Helena and there are considerably less than a thousand of them in existence. This makes it one of the rarest birds in the world. The turtle-dove (little barren-ground dove) was introduced from south-east Asia in the early 1700s. The pheasants were introduced by the Portuguese in the 1500s and so are the earliest imported birds. These are ring-necked pheasants. Red cardinals are related to the weaver birds of Africa and Swainson's canaries are an introduced species from South Africa, both having appeared on St Helena in the 1700s. As regards the moorhens, these remain a complete mystery to me. This list covers all the land birds on the island except for pigeons which are common on St Helena and of the type found the world over, more or less. They appear to have been brought from Europe in the mid-1800s.

With occasional rainfall occurring during the morning, nothing much was attempted until the afternoon, by which time the last of the previous night's fishing party had arisen – Nolan at 12.20. By this time the sun was beating down strongly and other than a walk through the woods to the local shop we did not cover a lot of ground. What we did notice was that a fair number of plants and bushes were now bearing new flowers. One I had not noticed before here on St Helena was a straightforward privet. In all this luxuriant growth, this was a plant I had not reckoned with.

It was far more straggly than its European cousins, but that was because it had been allowed to run wild.

It does appear that just about anything will grow on this island. The rain reasserted itself in the evening, so we decided enough was enough and saw it out playing cards.

9 February

This was a day never to be forgotten. Up well before 7 a.m. in order to go to Man and Horse to join in the monthly sheep round-up. What happens here is that – in our case – thirty people walk across country in a straight line driving everything in front of them, so that eventually all the sheep that live – basically wildly – on the hills, and probably do not see a human being from one month to the next, finish up in a pound, to be either remarked as regards ownership, checked as regards health, or even shorn if necessary. In some cases they are removed from the rest of the flock ready for the dinner table.

The isolation and ruggedness of this part of the island has to be seen to be believed. I consider it a privilege to have been invited to join this walk. After the walk and the various tasks have been completed, the participants take part in what can only be described as a 'blooming great booze-up'! Miles from anywhere, it is a fantastic event. After that is over and the beer and vodka are all gone, the ones that want to – I was included in this lot – then move on a few miles to the nearest village store and virtually buy them out of their stock of beer and sit outside it in order to supply the owners with plenty of empty bottles.

As I said before, this was a day never to be forgotten. The scenery can never be forgotten either. On the way out we left our vehicles overlooking Speery island. This is well covered in guano and is the place that trophy birds are most likely to be sighted. On around the hillsides along a five-foot track with a sheer drop down to our left to overlook Manati Bay, and then through a gate to rejoin the rugged sheep pastures and so to the sheep pound at the bottom of Water Gut. I would estimate that about three hundred sheep were involved in this round-up. As one of the Saints said to me after it was all over, 'I bet you thought you were walking off the map.'

My answer was, 'What do you mean, *thought?*'

10 February

A dullish morning by St Helena standards until about 11 a.m. when the sun began putting the pressure on. About 11.30 a.m., we took up an invitation to be shown around Plantation House – the governor's residence – and the grounds. This was very interesting. It is a lovely building and beautifully kept, as are the gardens. We met up with Jonathan the tortoise with an estimated age of between one hundred and fifty and two hundred years old. There were another five tortoises that we saw there as well as him. All except one were giants.

From here we went to the museum in Jamestown but that proved to be a fruitless journey as it was closed. My fault – I should have checked before going there. It was then that we saw our first actual accident occur on the island when a car and a motorcycle collided. I suppose it has to happen sometimes.

On the way back we saw a lovely stand of hollyhocks growing wild near the arboretum – there always seems to be something different to see here.

One oddity today. It did not rain at all, even during the nighttime.

There are a lot of rabbits living wild on St Helena, so this evening it was decided to get a couple for the dinner table. Only five cartridges could be found but they resulted in four rabbits being used for food. They are a useful supplement to the islanders' diet as wages here are a long way behind those in the UK and yet all imported things – food included – are more expensive. Cigarettes are cheaper, but one cannot live on cigarettes. Economics apart, rabbits in the wild do cause extensive erosion, something the island can well do without.

11 February

Really hot today. Summer seems to be here with a vengeance. To back this statement up, we have discovered a wasp's nest in the garden near to the chicken coop. Will leave it a couple of days but will probably have to get the Agriculture and Forestry Department people to deal with it eventually.

Had a very idle morning as it was so very hot. Wasps got worse, so did telephone for help. They were here within the hour and did the job efficiently. As I've said before, they are a useful unit. If anything, the afternoon got hotter. For anyone who enjoys the sunshine this is definitely the place to be.

Tomorrow is my birthday! All or most of the people I was with the day before yesterday made sure it was a day none of us would forget. We sat at the roadside with more drink than was sensible and we drank the evening away. It sounds bad, but in actual fact we had a great time. The road here is so quiet that not one vehicle passed us, and it is so remote that no one was within earshot anyway.

12 February

Got up with a hangover. It serves me right.

This turned out to be a lovely day. Presents and cards from home to begin with, then we called at Dillon's where I received more cards and a large birthday cake – probably the first one I have had done for me since I was a child – then we went on to the Consulate Hotel, where there was a performance with more cards, and, would you believe it, another large birthday cake. I must be doing something right. Later, it was back to Dillon's where we all had a convivial evening and got well into one of the cakes. Rounded the night off by going to the Police Social Club at the top of Ladder Hill. What a marvellous community of people these Saints are.

One bit of video camera recording that we did in the early evening that I am pleased about is the complete car journey from Blue Hill village into Jamestown, rounding it off with the harbour as dusk was arriving. That is something to cherish.

13 February

Up at the crack of dawn with the partridges shouting their heads off, with a backing from the mynah birds and canaries. I've noticed that there are even more flowers in bloom now. The dahlias are really multiplying and I've seen elder flowers for the first time since leaving England. By half past eight, the hills are ablaze with sunshine.

Spent the largest part of the morning in the woods insect hunting. The challenge of course is the reputedly extinct earwig. It was considered so officially in the 1960s, but when you see all the rotting tree trunks, etc. in the woodlands it is hard to accept in one's mind that there are not one or two somewhere. I found numerous cockroaches, different species of spider and beetle in the roots and bark of the deadwood but no earwigs. There is plenty of evidence of the white-ant or termite.

Their history has been one of plague to St Helenans. A slave ship was captured and broken up in 1840 and the slaves either returned to their homes or allowed to remain on the island. However it transpired that white ants were in its timbers and they eventually increased to disastrous levels. The Royal Navy was curing one evil, but had stumbled on another one. The termites have caused untold damage in the one hundred and fifty plus years since then, even eating the houses of the islanders. Fortunately they are now being held in check by the introduction of a termite-resistant timber called 'Iroko' that is rock hard and is used for building. It is almost like metal to handle, and has been a Godsend to these people.

14 February

It's the turn of the turtle doves to do the early morning calling today – perhaps the fact that it is St Valentine's day is the reason. It was another lovely day with the sunshine well established by 9 a.m., and yet I am feeling quite morose today, or perhaps the word is guilty.

I look around at all these friendly people and I can feel and see the despair of some of them caused by my own country's politicians. The island deserves a better deal than it is getting. Many get less than £30 a week and they are in work, not idling on the dole, yet food is more expensive if imported, as much of it is, than in the UK. St Helena was a most useful and strategic outpost for Britain in years gone by, helping in unlocking the key to the orient to our merchants, leading on to the settling of Australia, New Zealand, etc. Now it is given a background position *par excellence*. Even the French government faced up to their responsibility by giving the little island off Canada named St Pierre Et Miquelon, with a population of 5,000, over twice as much cash as we give to St Helena, and on top of that they get a full French passport which, in turn, gives them common market rights to work in the UK.

Let's face it, there are only 5,500 St Helenans, far less than the attendance of a third division football match. Surely we can do something practical, especially when one thinks of the vast numbers of people who still arrive in the UK and do not even attempt to learn our language, never mind work for a living. This island has been neglected ever since the opening of the Suez Canal, and let us face up to it, its smallness is undoubtedly why there is just no kudos to be won by the politicians for siding with these people who are probably more English in their unconscious attitude to life than we are.

That is enough about politics, it is not really my forte.

The whole of the day turned out to be filled with birdsong and sunshine, and when it is like that, then the headlands, which stand like huge fortresses under siege by the sea, really do look so very serene and inviting. This island is a magnificent place to see. As I've said before, mere words cannot hope to do it credit. Come here and see it for yourself.

When you have so many different things to see, time goes by all too swiftly. It is my belief that only people of slow moving minds could ever get bored on this lovely little isle.

15 February

High winds and low clouds early on but nice pleasant sunshine by 8.30 a.m. (I am told it is raining in England).

I had a telephone call from the headmistress of the Jamestown Palling middle school, Rita Nichols, informing me that not only had the education officer contacted her about the proposed pen pal and school link-up with the Banbury Hardwick school, but that fifty-one children had put their names down on the list that she had posted on the notice board at the school. All have now written and their letters will be *en route* to England via Ascension Island on the ship that sails this Sunday, all in the same envelope supplied by the school, with a covering letter from her to the headmaster. That is what I call co-operation. Let's hope all of the children in each country benefit in some way.

On a walk in late afternoon around High Peak, we found several dogwood trees growing. This is of a different natural order to all the other endemic plants of the island, and is in flower. These are small, greenish-white, and are on the end of stems in clusters. I had quite a feeling of achievement in finding and recognising this tree, although it appears, I am told, on the peaks and ridges in reasonable numbers.

16 February

This was the day for doing the round the island trip. It began in Jamestown and left by the road known as Side Path, which is on the east side of the valley, looking across it at Ladder Hill. The road rose steadily through the scrub, aloes and prickly pears until it arrived at the aptly named Button-up Corner. After this there is a very sharp bend by Alarm Cottage and then a whole new countryside opens up.

One can now see Longwood Gate and the tall trees around Longwood Old House and also see deep down into Sane Valley. Over to the left stands Flagstaff Hill – 2,257 feet high – and the slightly lower bulk called the Barn. At this point we stopped for about fifteen minutes for anyone who wanted to walk to Napoleon's tomb. St Helena's main historical property is a couple of miles around the aptly named Devil's Punch Bowl and then along an avenue of trees to a sentry box. The French government maintain the property.

We then went back to Hutt's Gate and its quaint store, then around the peaks on the north side, with their adjoining beautiful pastures and forests and crossed a ridge to behold the fantastic sight of the south side of the island. This is Sandy Bay country, and anyone who has ever seen it can never ever forget it. It is here you see the monoliths named Lot, Lot's Wife and the Asses' Ears, and the volcanic wasteland – yet so awesome – that is the Gates of Chaos and the Devil's Garden.

Then another transformation as we saw another aptly named spot, Mount Pleasant. This is totally opposite to what we had just left and it is very green with a feeling of peace about it. There is an old flax mill in the distance.

We moved on along Sandy Bay ridge with its flax protecting us from a vertigo attack to Plantation House for a halt in the grounds of the governor's residence. It is a lovely house in grounds surrounded by mature trees, and is home to at least six quite large tortoises. You can also see St Paul's Cathedral at Whitegate from here through the trees.

Moving on again, but now nearing Jamestown, we went below High Knoll, through Half Tree Hollow and so to the top of Jacob's Ladder, then down Ladder Road into upper Jamestown, on down to the Market Hall and so into Main Street, past the castle and on to the wharf.

This was a great day out, and I would suggest no one should fail to take it. Should you wish to try it for yourself and are limited for time, it can be booked at the purser's office on the RMS.

17 February

Visited Plantation House – again. The previous time we had been invited we had not brought the video camera, but this time we did bring it and got some good film footage, thanks to the full co-operation of the girls on duty. Everywhere we go, we get genuine help by people who are quite happy to give it to us.

We then did some shopping in Jamestown, and while doing this were handed a printed invitation for a social evening for 4 March at the Blue Lamp, which is the St Helena Police Club.

Next, we video filmed some of Jamestown, including Jacob's Ladder, and some of Half Tree Hollow. After that the evening was fast approaching so we returned home.

We did see in the harbour during the afternoon the boat that is on a voyage circumnavigating the globe. It certainly looks very small for a voyage like that, being only eighteen feet long.

On the way back to Blue Hill we saw many rabbits in and around the roadsides, especially along the ridge that runs from High Peak to Thomson's Wood. Still on a wild animal theme, having arrived and turned on the radio, we heard that the Agriculture and Forestry Commission had captured seventeen wild donkeys in one determined swoop. These they are prepared to sell them to islanders for £50 each for work purposes if not already name tagged. If any are name tagged, then their owners are in trouble.

I was given some wild guavas to taste. I have never tried them before, and although not as pleasing to the mouth as granadillas, are nevertheless quite acceptable. I was then given some cultivated ones which are undoubtedly better.

18 February

Started off the day by going to High Point to look around the nursery shop (horticulture). It has the best selection of pot plants on the island. Then it was on past Guinea Grass, where they are building a skittle alley in the community centre, and on to Ladder Hill and into Jamestown, where I purchased some first day covers from the post office and also did some additional shopping. A couple of drinks in the Standard followed before carrying on to the arboretum.

Here I found one or two trees worthy of mention. They were the she-cabbage tree, the he-cabbage tree and the gumwood. The arboretum is a plantation of trees especially planted out in 1977 to celebrate the silver anniversary of Queen Elizabeth II's accession to the throne, as a sign at the entrance proclaims. It is laid out as a country walk, very tastefully and naturally done. Again, here is something that the island visitor just should not miss. One should not miss anything really!

We spent the evening trying out the tapes and films that we have produced to date and then, after trapping a lizard in the beam of the torch for a few moments on an outside wall, it was time for bed.

19 February

A small problem this morning – a rat in the chicken coop. Actually this is not as bad as it seems. Around here there are none of the brown or sewer rats – which have been virtually exterminated here. What is here is a cream-bellied tree rat, which is fairly widespread. It is a long-tailed variety and – although still a pest – is not at all likely to enter houses and is very unlikely to transmit any disease as it is very fastidious in its cleaning and grooming and is very secretive and shy. However, poison is put down for these rodents because of the damage they do. After all, at the end of the day they are officially classified as pests.

About 10 a.m., we went on a particularly lovely walk that involved going up and then down the other side of Thompson's Hill, into Thompson's Valley, the cattle pastures of the churchyard – not really one, but so named because of the resemblance to gravestones of the boulders strewn around – and on to Ball Alley with its high-powered trade winds almost permanently blowing a dust storm between the Devil's Cap and Hooper's Ridge. To the right-hand side is Manati Bay and Speery Island.

The island is renowned for two species of bird that actually nest on it, the sooty tern and the Madeir – a storm petrel – but I must confess I saw neither. This is the Gates of Chaos countryside. From here on the view of Sandy Bay below us was stunning. At Horse Ridge, I looked back across to Distant Cottage which again is well named, as it is so far from any other dwelling, and could clearly see the three foot high St Helena plantain. It is a giant compared to other plantains and is endemic to the island. It was then on to Old Lufkins, which is an old ruined house that has become a landmark. It was built in the 1680s. Next came Bamboo Hedge, then up and up through the flax as we again reached the peak of Thompson's Hill. After a short rest, it was all downhill back into Blue Hill.

Later in the day, on the way into Jamestown by car, I saw the first cock pheasant I have seen on the island and a little further on a hen pheasant, near to the turn-off to Plantation House.

One place we did not visit – but must – on Horse Ridge, is the Norman Williams Nature Reserve. We got as far as the gateway to it and read the WWF plaque just inside it, but did not actually enter... There is time yet.

20 February

There is a local saying here, 'Sun before seven, rain by eleven'. Well, that has proved true today. It was lovely early on, but later rain fell. This suits me well, but warnings are being broadcast over the local radio of the imminence of a drought. The island's gardeners want more rain. During the early afternoon, in blazing sunshine – we must be mad – we walked along to High Hill and tackled it. On reaching the summit, we found precisely what we had not expected. Amongst the thinly clad fir-tree roots, prickly pears were growing. The textbooks say that this should not occur. This has to be the result of random bird droppings (the prickly pears, not the textbook).

A couple of hours were spent chopping down the aloe trees from around the garden area in order that they could be utilised as boundary poles when placed horizontally around the outer limits.

At 5.15 p.m. I watched the RMS making her way out towards Ascension from the valley in Blue Hill. Any mail she is carrying to the rest of the world will be airmailed out of Ascension to the UK. It will take her two days to reach Ascension.

21 February

It is very noticeable now that the mynah birds are fetching and carrying pieces of paper and other materials that they intend to build their nests in the greenery at the base of the aloe trees. It is midsummer here, by which season the birds in most countries will have, in all probability, ceased breeding but these mynahs are different, the seasons not coming into their planning at all.

On the third of this month we had been to St Paul's Cathedral in Whitegate, so today decided to look at one or two others. Religion is certainly well catered for on St Helena, as the churches that we saw and took note of were St James's and St John's, both in Jamestown and St Matthew's at Hutt's Gate, all Church of England. This latter one was build originally to receive worshippers from Longwood in one direction and Levelwood from the other. It so happens that they both have their own ones now. There is also St Martin's in the woods at High Point. At Half Tree Hollow is the largest New Apostolic Church, built at a cost in excess of £200,000 – that is a lot of money out here – and there are Baptist chapels to be found at Head O'Wain, Sandy Bay and at Knollcombes. This last one has a burial ground on the side of the hill where some Boer prisoners found their final resting place.

The Baptists are led by a minister appointed from South Africa, as indeed are the Anglicans, as St Helena is a diocese in the ecclesiastical province of South Africa. Also, commissioned by the South African Salvation Army, is a captain who lives with his wife in a small set of rooms against their headquarters in Jamestown. They have a fair number of followers throughout the island. There was for many years a soup kitchen run by the Salvation Army, but that is no longer there. The site has been re-developed as a supermarket, in Half Tree Hollow.

There is a small church in upper Jamestown for Roman Catholics. Other than these traditional churches, there are also

Jehovah's Witnesses, Seventh Day Adventists, Bahai and Mormons.

As I said, religion is well catered for here.

Late in the day, we learned that a sloop has arrived in the harbour that is carrying a party of adults (crew and teachers) and youngsters, who are being taught how to handle such a boat. The nationalities involved are Finnish and Polish. The boat is two years old. In 1992, it came third out of two hundred ships in the Tall Ships Race. The name of this vessel is the *Fryderyle Chopin*, and is registered in Poland.

22 February

Drought was the worry before today, but now it has rained almost incessantly causing small rivulets to cascade down the pathways of the hillsides. Unable to venture out at one stage of the day, I took to looking at the maps I have. To begin with, St Helena is shown simply as an 'inset island'. It is so far out in the Atlantic Ocean, many miles from either South America or Africa that it appears only in a box in a convenient space on the page. As a result, the ordinary holiday seeker, or for that matter the map reader, just does not know what is being missed. This small island is a veritable scenic paradise.

Late morning, we went to a house at Barren Ground to get some bananas, and although it was – as I said – still only morning, the elderly lady who lives alone there insisted on supplying me with a largish glass of whisky... and then another. The Saints are people with hearts of gold, whatever they have they are prepared to share, and they are not the world's richest people by a long way. Another lady gave us a bag of peaches. During the afternoon, with the rain abating somewhat, I cleared a blocked drainpipe that was giving trouble and then in the evening met up with 'The Shepherds'. Result... oblivion.

23 February

The sun came back this morning. The mynahs have resumed their nest building and the whole of the valley is alive and vibrant.

We did take a bit of a walk during the morning, but as it was so very hot we did not go very far and returned to base until mid-afternoon. Later, we went firstly to the top of Thompson's Hill and then on along the Sandy Bay ridge as far as High Peak. The weather here was quite astonishing. To the seaward side of Sandy Bay, nothing was visible through the thickly swirling clouds, but on the other side of the self-same ridge, the sun was shining brightly. It was like this for several hours. It really is something that you have to see for yourself to believe.

At night-time we had a full moon which was most pleasant, and even as late as 2.15 a.m. – when I killed the last mosquito of the night – it was virtually as clear as daylight outside.

24 February

Got up to a rainstorm at 7 a.m., but fortunately, by 8.30 a.m. it had ceased as at 8.45 we had booked a taxi to take us to Black Gate to commence a walk from there at 9.30. For this walk – which continued one way and another until 4 p.m. – the weather was absolutely perfect, as indeed was the whole of the walk in all its aspects.

The morning part of the walk was from Black Gate, up along the flax alongside the meadow and then along a lovely easy track until it dropped into a pasture. Once a house and stable had stood here, but from time to time it had been visited by persons requiring building materials from it, so that now virtually none of it remained. In the pasture, a couple of dozen cattle in perfect condition were chewing the cud, and right in the centre of the meadow was a really well-fruited cherry tree that had once belonged to the house.

On the hillside, we espied some chow-chows growing on a bank and picked a few to take for cooking. Eventually we emerged at Silver Hill Bar, where we purchased beer and biscuits and took a rest before continuing from there up to the flax mill at Rock Rose past a plant that I think will remain in my memory for ever, a really beautiful wild ginger plant in full flower. The mill is now a ruined shell of a building but was obviously of importance in its time. We went on a little way and took in some fantastic scenery, especially two outcrops, one of which resembled a gorilla's head and the other a resting sea cow. The whole of this scenic tableau is now an indelible memory. This particular day must rank as number one. Other days may equal, but none can ever surpass it.

25 February

For anyone who thinks he can walk, then this really was the day. Setting off at 6.45 a.m., I walked from Blue Hill village into the centre of Jamestown. The nine and a half mile walk took a full three and a half hours, which is quite good considering the hills involved, and then after a day in town, and due to a misunderstanding – my fault – about the return journey plans, I walked up all 699 steps of Jacob's Ladder and on up the winding sloping road through Half Tree Hollow out to Plantation House before getting a lift for the rest of the journey. I don't think I will ever try this again.

After experiencing this, I was then expected to return to Jamestown for a quiet convivial evening to round things off. This I did, but as a matter of fact, I do not honestly believe that I have ever suffered physically so much for so little in all of my life. Having said that, though, I must say that the evening was still a very pleasant one, which is the way of St Helena.

26 February

Yet another lovely morning to wake up to. It really is a case of 'Stop the world, I want to get off'.

Spent the morning locally. The gardens are now looking splendid with good fresh vegetables, greens and tomatoes, in some quantities. There was a white, black and yellow striped garden spider on its web among the chillies. It must have been about two inches in body length with a leg span of about five inches. Quite a giant. The web had several insects trapped in it. Also, we found an eight inch long hawkworm, bright yellow and several shades of green. This will one day change into a death's-head moth, which can be quite large.

Late afternoon we went into Jamestown and that was really a sight to behold at the sea wall, as the waves were extremely fierce and the whole area was like a thunderous battleground with sea and land meeting in stark confrontation. There are no off-shore islands to buffer the shock waves that have been driven across the ocean in any of four directions. As they crashed into the wall, they rose up and over it to a general height of about twenty feet and more, occasionally quite a bit more. Stones and small rocks were strewn all around the sea wall on the landward side.

27 February

A lovely hot day again. After last evening's heavy seas, I had expected a storm, but that did not transpire.

The bulk of the day was taken up by visiting a family that live at Barren Ground – what an unfortunate name – who really did treat us marvellously. As with virtually all Saints, it was a privilege to meet them.

When we arrived at their cottage the sweat was literally running off us, it was so hot. They immediately gave us ice-cold drinks and then, when we were at a more reasonable temperature they plied us with sandwiches, biscuits and a couple of glasses of whisky. Just imagine this situation anywhere else – it wouldn't happen, would it?

By the time we had walked back to Blue Hill village dusk had fallen. Another pleasant day. At night-time, with the full moon still in the sky, what was almost daylight returned, especially during the small hours. Looking from the bedroom window across the valley drenched in moonlight is a great experience. Looking up along the ridge can play havoc with the mind in this volcanic setting.

28 February

Today we walked from 7.45 in the morning, going from Blue Hill via Hutt's Gate almost to Silver Hill before diverting to the beautiful countryside that skirts that area before eventually moving on the Levelwood, by which time we were well and truly worn out. There where several examples of the beautiful drooping sweet-scented ladies' petticoat (moon flowers) on this walk. They really are lovely. This part of the island is totally unsurpassable. It is absolutely impossible to explain how beautiful this place is, so I will not even try to do it. Words are totally inadequate. Perfection is perfection wherever one finds it and here it is. Why St Helena has to be such a small island, I will never even begin to comprehend. It is perfection. I really do have to return.

The longer we remain on the island, the harder it will be to leave. Among the cultivated flowers were some exquisite fuchsias; I picked and pressed one just for future reference.

From this point, I looked across directly at Sugar Loaf which stands exactly where the original volcano erupted eleven million years ago, and to Great Stone Top and Little Stone Top, which are more recently formed volcanic rocks made of trachyte instead of basalt. Trachyte, because of its high viscosity, moves far slower than basalt and consequently the lava has congregated near to its eruption points, hence the two 'Tops'. Great Stone Top is St Helena's highest cliff, being at the top of a four hundred metre drop. Standing at this point and looking at this landscape, and then turning around and looking at the greenery of the steep hillsides immediately facing it is like being on two different islands at the same time. This of course is part of the charm of St Helena.

One thing worthy of comment that I saw just beyond Windy Ridge flax mill, was two workers in charge of about a dozen donkeys walking along the roadway, off to do some wood cutting.

They looked as though they really did mean business with the packs already on the animals' backs.

1 March

A very high wind blowing early this morning, but no rain.

I have noticed that quite a lot of honeysuckle and also cow parsley is now appearing in flower. These are both typically British plants, but they are thriving in this environment. Most plants do seem to succeed here, but perhaps the gorse and the New Zealand flax are too successful, as they are now proving almost impossible to eradicate. The flax industry was important to the island's economy at one time, but with the advent of synthetic materials it became obsolete and despite a period of prosperity during the Second World War, it collapsed totally in 1966. Its only redeeming features now are that it can be used as a supplementary cattle food, albeit of low nutritional value, and as scenic greenery to ward off vertigo around the cliffs and ridges of the island. Other than as a fuel, gorse is even less useful.

During the afternoon the rainstorm that had been threatening all day did happen. It was not a really exceptional one, but nevertheless did keep us indoors all the while until about five o'clock, and then within an hour it started again. This time the wind was accompanying it, together with low scudding cloud cover, so we decided to simply stay in and watch the video and also play cards. This was a day that got away.

2 March

Still low cloud cover during the morning with strong winds.

Went into Jamestown during the late morning and early afternoon on business, and while there I was given a couple of mangoes to taste. Not my favourite food. It was on this trip into Jamestown that I realised just how large and imposing the Jehovah's Witness Hall in Half Tree Hollow is. They also have a largish one at Levelwood.

Another church that I have not previously mentioned but that we passed on this journey is the one for Blue Hill, the Anglican St Helena and the Cross.

We had visitors later on, so we did not move from the house after that. The only other thing to mention for this day is that we received two goats on the premises this afternoon for fattening up. They should keep the grass down. Throughout the night very strong winds prevailed, together with a couple of sharp rainstorms.

3 March

I've never seen rain quite like we had early this morning from about seven o'clock until nine o'clock. Actually, it was a pleasant experience and really freshened the island up. Then the rain stopped and although the cloud cover remained on the hilltops all around the island, it became very good – if somewhat humid – walking weather. At Watercress Bridge I saw my first fully-flowered arum lily and nearby both St John's lilies and cannas, together with some lovely pink watsonias.

Between Levelwood and Green Hill, one passes through what is undoubtedly the most scenic area you could wish for: a few ups and downs along the winding road past clumps of wild ginger and a really pleasant mulberry tree next to the large Norfolk pine, past hillsides of cattle and of sheep amongst the furze bushes and on to the picnic trestles at the top of Green Hill for a thirty-minute well-earned sit down with some chocolate and crackers. It was most enjoyable. The reverse journey was punctuated with many stops to view and admire what may have been missed on the way out. We even found a culvert full of tadpoles.

There is one particular stand of about fifty eucalyptus trees that are capable of holding one almost spellbound. Yes, if there is any casting of spells to be done, this is the island for it and this is the spot for it; I found it utterly enchanting. The next place along the road beyond Green Hill is Fairyland. We decided to leave that for another day, although I did have an initiation for this when I was shown how to wave a white handkerchief just below a passing fairy tern – which bird gives Fairyland its name – and then see it cruise and flutter to weigh up what was going on, coming in quite low in the process. Obviously this is a bit of fun that a lot of Saints are clever at.

One thing that I learned today was that the rock I had referred to on 24 February as resembling a sleeping sea cow is actually named Elephant Rock. I was nearly right, wasn't I?

4 March

The weather this morning was what could be described as reasonable, turning to lovely sunshine at about ten o'clock, whilst I am told that the other side of the island was covered in thick clouds. This is a thing worth mentioning about St Helena. Although it is small, one can get two or even three different weather conditions prevailing on it at the same time, sun in one area, rain in another and either just dull or fair in another. Jamestown, the capital, being in a deep valley at sea level, is usually the most humid spot, whilst up in the hillside villages it is more usually fresh and pleasant for walking. The scenery everywhere is unbeatable regardless of the weather.

There is a peculiar shrub growing in fair quantities under High Peak that I have been unable to name as it is unlike anything I have ever seen before. Enquiries revealed that it is a hybrid (ebony and redwood) that was discovered for the very first time in February, 1983 in five seedlings after seed had been collected from ebony trees and had been planted next to redwoods. These hybrids are far healthier that either of their parents inasmuch as they are larger and more upstanding than they. This hybrid does make a lovely hardy garden shrub. I am told that the cross pollination of the two trees in all probability occurred with the aid of the imported honey bees, otherwise some endemic insects would have done it years ago.

Late on in the afternoon the heavens opened and the rain was most spectacular, but there was a dodgy side to this. We had a visitor – the local fruiterer – who brought some mangoes and stayed to talk for a couple of hours. The road here is of earth, not tarmac, and after churning it up quite spectacularly he got completely bogged down. A Land Rover from the garage in Jamestown had to be sent for to get him out. It can be quite funny if it is not you that it is happening to. Eventually the rain cleared and we went into town for a drink at the Consulate Hotel and then on to a social evening at the police club.

5 March

This was a day with a difference and no mistake about it. A beautiful, hot, sunny morning saw us making tracks into Jamestown, where we attended a wedding ceremony at 11 a.m. in the castle. From the castle we all went to Ann's Pantry in the municipal gardens for champagne and snacks together with the reception party and then to the Oakland's Hotel for a lovely well-presented barbecue and totally unlimited drinks coupled with one or two impromptu speeches and the inevitable ribaldry. From start to finish, we were involved with the festivities for about nine hours in all. It was an excellent day blessed with good weather.

In the gardens of the Oakland's Hotel stands a healthy avocado tree, a small banana grove and many other interesting plants, but what took my fancy the most was some really strong-scented rosemary. As in a lot of St Helena gardens – and growing wild for that matter – there were plenty of freesias, fuchsias and agapanthus as well as garden roses. This is a very nice spot for such a celebration, and we enjoyed every minute of it.

6 March

I have a book in my possession entitled *The Endemic Flora of St Helena; a Struggle for Survival* and in it I had already read about the St Helena rosemary. Having yesterday seen the rosemary at the Oakland's Hotel it crossed my mind this morning that they might be the same plant. The book does state that the endemic one can be found growing wild at High Hill, so we went there to see if we could find any. We did. The two plants are only slightly different from each other but the St Helena one is more of a grey–green in foliage than the English one, and what we found was more straggly, although of course, this may be due to soil conditions. I am told that quite a few young plants are being raised at the nursery in Scotland.

As we were here looking for an endemic plant we decided to look farther for any other kind and were fortunate enough to find one, although it was probably the most common one of all. The shrub-wood is low to the ground about three feet or less in height, but with quite a large diameter and bearing pretty little white flowers something like daisy heads in appearance. Instead of a yellow centre, there is a mauve to purple colour.

With the weather being none-too-clever until about 5.30 in the evening, we did not do very much else today other than catching the donkey ready for his journey down to the beach tomorrow, where he will be expected to carry any fish that are caught by the fishing party during the early hours back up to Blue Hill. I will not be with them.

7 March

Heavy rain during the night was followed by a lovely day. Despite the night's rain the fishing party departed from Blue Hill via Ebony Plain at six o'clock in near darkness, making for the rocks at Thompson's Valley, complete with the donkey.

For myself it was a day for walking, basically based on the spot called Alice's Point at the gateway to Diana's Peak. This is a beautiful spot to watch the sun appear over the horizon and I actually saw my favourite St Helena wildflower, the ginger lily, awaken and open right up as it was caressed by the warm sunlight. There were a number of grass frogs about that could have been the parents of the tadpoles seen four days ago as we were within a mile of that spot, and over to one side, just away from the pathway, were some luxuriant growths of yams and wild mango. The yams are regularly found in most of the guts (gut is the local word for a small stream) and years ago were cultivated to such an extent that the word yamstocks came into the dictionary to name the people who tended them. Wild celery is also here; this is edible but usually very tough. The ginger lily is similar to the ginger root plant that supplies us with spice but in this case it is inedible. I know this for a fact.

The sun became very hot just after midday, so it was a picnic lunch of beer, whisky and biscuits followed by an hour in the Land of Nod on the hillside. What a life! What an island! I really could stay here for ever and ever. A nice leisurely walk back down to Silver Hill completed the day.

Meanwhile, back to the fishing party. They had returned to Blue Hill at about five o'clock and it was immediately obvious why they had taken the donkey with them. The amount of fish that they had caught could in no way have been carried home by them otherwise, especially along that three foot wide track up on Ebony Plain with the vertiginous drop at the side of it. What they had caught amounted to seventeen large jacks, four conger eels, two fivefingers, one old wife and four greenfish. This was adequate fish to keep a family for well over a month, being more than forty pounds in weight.

I got sunburned today – I never thought I would experience that again.

8 March

Very humid today, so we restricted ourselves to just walking down the gut at the bottom of Dick's Valley below High Hill. Even the birds seemed to be missing today because of the stillness in the air.

I suppose we really did need a reasonably quiet day today after the excitement of yesterday, so it did not come amiss. I did do a little reading to keep up with facts and figures, and one set of such figures I found interesting were the dates on which the three South Atlantic islands became what they now are. They are:

In April 1834 St Helena became a crown colony.

In 1922 Ascension became a dependency of St Helena.

In 1938 Tristan Da Cunha became a dependency of St Helena.

Another fact I uncovered is that the two old peepul trees on the north-east corner of Main Street outside the Canister (built 1959), which I have referred to previously, are the self same ones that slaves were formerly sold under before the Royal Navy crushed the trade. Posters of yesteryear advertising slaves for sale 'under the trees' are actually on display at the Canister at the top of the stairs in the Education Department Offices.

Whilst talking about the premises of the Canister, I should mention that it also contains the St Helena Handicraft Association shop where the visitor can purchase locally produced lacework, embroidery, shopping baskets, books, banana leaf hats, aloe fibre mats and wood inlay items. It is well worth a look around. Another item of interest is the coaster type product made from thorn-tree seeds.

9 March

The birds are singing again. The air is fresh and the sun is shining.

That line I wrote down at eight o'clock this morning. As the day wore on, it improved, if anything. It is so remote here that for anyone of a like mind to myself who appreciates tranquillity it is ideal. There are no buses, no trains, in fact no public transport of any kind. Except for cars and a very few taxis, there are no motorised vehicles at all, but basically this is adequate as most journeys are very local, the farthest village from anywhere being Blue Hill, which is where I am staying. As I have already recorded, on 25 February I walked all the way into Jamestown and virtually all the way back, sandwiching a day about town in between. In fact, no car ever came to St Helena until 1929 when an Austin 7 was brought over under the Ordinance (motor) of 1928, which authorised the import of motor vehicles. This led to the surfacing of roads and now there must be almost a thousand vehicles on the island, of which the vast majority must be in Jamestown itself and in Half Tree Hollow, most of which are in all probability only used for ridiculously short local journeys. Most are simply between these two communities.

About 10.30 a.m., we set off on the long walk up Thompson's Hill, along Ebony Plain and down into Thompson's Valley. I had heard so much from the fishing party about how good that walk was I decided to try it for myself. In the write-up two days ago, I described the ledge to be traversed as being about three feet wide over a vertiginous drop. That was wrong. In most places it was struggling to be two feet wide. It was quite an experience, although I must admit I did enjoy it. I think it was about 2.30 p.m. when we returned, not having stopped anywhere. Four hours' solid walking along cliff edges.

In the course of three days I have been sunburned on both legs, stubbed my big toe, grazed my right knee and spiked my shoulder in a couple of places on an aloe stick. It's like being on the front line. Even so, I am still entirely happy with everything about the island. I had been to sixty-seven different countries and islands prior to coming to St Helena, and none can even begin to compare with it. With so much travelling under my belt I believe I am entitled to this opinion. If you have the cash and the time and are reasonably fit, try it for yourself.

10 March

Out very early this morning – 6.45 a.m. Saw two moorhens down by Bishop's Bridge near the stream in amongst the various lilies growing there. Very pleasing to the eye. It was then on through the lovely lanes to Hutt's Gate, Black Gate and Silver Hill and on to Levelwood and literally under the shade of Sugar Loaf while the sun blazed down. Erosion is rife here, but nonetheless green patches are appearing where apparently there were none not too many years ago. Some parts, however, appear to be past saving although they are very eye-catching with their different hues ranging from black to red to orange to ochre to yellow and blue/grey. The flax problem that I am told they once had in this area seems to have been eradicated, although it has made way in several places for patches of aloe, cactus and prickly pears.

Up here and on Great Stone Top it is incredible, but nevertheless true, to say that wild rabbits eke out an existence. Just off the coast at Great Stone Top Bay are the two islands named Shore and George. Both the masked booby and the brown booby nest there. Both are specialists at diving for food and the masked is the larger of the two. The names they have got – other than the obvious – is because of how easily they are robbed of their catches of fish by the marauding frigate birds.

Some of the gardens in Levelwood and Silver Hill are perfect examples of what can be done given loving care and attention by owners who know just what they are doing. They are a credit to them. Potatoes and tomatoes are growing healthily in some confusion and profusion. There are lots of chickens hereabouts, a fair smattering of goats, and even a few sheep. The people here will not go hungry. There are even one or two little cottage industries that I found quite amazing.

11 March

Another hot morning. I went out into the local forestry area alone with a view to finding any plants that I might previously have missed. One tree that I had missed before, would you believe it, was an ordinary oak tree. It was nothing like the size of an English one, I hasten to add. There are lots of ripe blackberries around and also many lovely double pink-red camellias along the roadside and also lots of hibiscus. Other than these, there is a veritable yellow carpet of everlasting flowers with quite a number of butterflies flittering around them. Both the turtle doves and the chukar partridges can be heard calling all around me and the ethereal fairy terns are keeping me company. As ever, the mynahs are here.

About 1.30 p.m., a fair pleasing breeze blew up to accompany the very hot sunshine which certainly made for very good conditions, although on the debit side I did notice a number of wasps about, but after a while they disappeared. I was quite pleased about that.

On returning to Blue Hill, I was told that the waste pipe from the kitchen was blocked. This I had to strip down, clean and then reassemble. The job was successful, but was something I could have done without in this temperature. As the saying goes about five foot high magistrates: 'These little things are sent to try us'.

This brought me to evening time by which time the sun was setting. We then decided to go for a drive, but as we went round an S bend outside the St Helena and the Cross church, we met a heavy lorry with a full load of breeze blocks heading straight for us. We braked and came to a full stop; he braked, but his brakes locked and he came head-on into us, actually pushing us backward by a little way. There was quite extensive damage to the bodywork by the look of it, but fortunately no one was injured.

After the police had cleared the road and finished their paperwork it was jet black with no stars and low cloud cover. The vehicles were sent to Half Tree Hollow government garage, and we walked home in the opposite direction. At no point did we actually see the road it was so very dark. That was quite an eerie walk, to say the very least.

12 March

This morning we set off from Pine Gate. What a lovely spot to begin a walk from. Music was blasting up from the valley below from someone's radio and we found it a pleasing accompaniment. Morning glory and wild ginger lilies were all around us as we made our way towards Green Hill. There was also plenty of busy Lizzy in full bloom, and around one particular cottage someone had been occupied cutting back the ginger lilies... What a beautiful scent that made. Even now I am totally captivated by the ginger lily. And why not indeed?

It is so very quiet around this part of the island that other than some cattle, a few sheep and one donkey, we saw no other life at all except for about two dozen fairy terns, a few red cardinals and a couple of mynah birds. We saw only three cottages in about two miles and two of those were uninhabited, and only two vehicles passed us. All along this area on the right hand side when travelling from Green Hill was the vista of Lot and Lot's Wife and then farther on other such configurations of the landscape as we skirted around Sandy Bay's ridges, whilst on our left side we had high – very high hills covered mainly in flax, but some in trees. An artist would have a field day here, as indeed would a cameraman.

13 March

Out at 7.15 this morning and walked the four miles to White Gate where friends met us and drove us the remaining two and a half miles to Sandy Bay beach to take part in a picnic-barbecue. The scenery here is simply phenomenal.

While some were fishing and some were playing ball games, I busied myself walking up one or two guts leading from Broad Gut coming from the surrounding hills down to the sea. Although at this point it looks like a moonscape, it is a fact that quite a lot of plant life grows here. I saw sea holly, deadly nightshade, periwinkle (that's very pretty), prickly pears, lantana, St Helena samphire and also a night-blooming cactus. Each of these plants is scattered thinly around but nevertheless is there.

One succulent low growing plant of interest that I saw quite a number of was the endemic 'baby's toes', and there was also a type of mesembryanthemum which looked like an ice plant. Also, believe it or not, I found a tomato plant which I have since been told does produce edible baby tomatoes. It was growing wild on the side of one of the dried-up guts. As I said before, all this in a barren area that at first glance looks like a photograph of the moon's surface. There was also blueweed, wild mango and parsley.

I found what was a military parade ground particularly interesting. I would think that even a lot of Saints probably didn't know that. Here, partially buried in the compounded black sand and earth lie two eighteenth-century cannons that appear to have slipped and fallen from the cliffs above, and just to the right as you face them are a couple of blowholes where the sea does some astonishing visual effects as you stand watching it.

There is a type of bean that semi-fossilises and gets washed in on the Benguela current onto the beach that is supposed to bring good luck to whoever finds it. I looked and failed. Isn't it always the way? The journey back up from the beach to the ridges must be one of the most awe-inspiring views on earth.

Well fed, well watered and utterly worn out, we eventually returned to Blue Hill in total darkness. That was a full day.

14 March

This morning was a little overcast early on so I made it my business to find out what I could about the cannons and defensive fortifications that I saw yesterday at Sandy Bay. It transpired that they were built on the instructions of Governor Lambert in 1742. He designed one continuous line from Broad Gut to Sandy Bay Valley, but because of his impatience to speed up the completion of the job, he decided not to use any mortar. Speed he got, but unfortunately the wall had only a short life and no longer exists. He also fortified Horse's Head and Seale's Battery. These are also badly deteriorated ruins. This is in total contrast to the excellent military batteries that exist all around the coastline that undoubtedly kept marauding navies out of St Helena waters.

Another fact that I unearthed is that the first ship to be sunk in James Bay was the *Witte Leeuw* in 1613. She was one of four heavily armed Dutch vessels that attacked two Portuguese carracks which were standing at anchor in the bay. The Portuguese were commanded by Captain Don Geronimo de Almeida who not only drove off the more heavily armed Dutchmen, but actually sank the *Witte Leeuw* which was carrying porcelain that she was bringing back to Europe from the Dutch East Indies. Over the succeeding centuries, much of this porcelain has been washed up in James Bay.

With rain coming and lasting virtually the whole of the afternoon, it was a case of carrying on with the reading, and other facts that I have found out are that football is played on Sunday afternoons; that the central sports ground is on Francis Plain; there is a nine hole golf club at Longwood; and small bore rifle shooting is very popular, with the main club being in Jamestown at Castle Moat. In season, cricket is played on a Sunday, there is a rounders league; there is a swimming pool; and fishing is very popular. This should look after most sports-minded people.

15 March

Decided to have a day in town today. The weather was pleasant, so made the first stop at Cason's Gate at the arboretum where yesterday the governor and the bishop, together with a number of middle-school children, planted thirty endemic trees to celebrate Commonwealth Day, which is always on the second Monday in March. They are planted near to the roadway so that even a casual passer-by can see them. This makes everyone aware of them and some are real beauties, especially the two principal ones, the redwood and the gumwood.

As I've said before, the Agriculture and Forestry Commission is doing a marvellous job on this beautiful island.

It was then on to town for general shopping and a visit to Ann's Place and Dot's Café; a walk around the gardens with the fountain, fish ponds and flowers, each complementing the others amongst the fine old trees, with the turtle doves coo-cooing to whoever cared to listen; and then on to the wharf to see the small boats rocking at anchor on the calm sea.

I then went into St James's church and signed the visitor's book. If peace is what one wants, then here is where to find it. The actual church was built in 1765 and a spire was added a year later, but this was removed in 1982 as it was considered to have become unsafe. Christianity has been practised in buildings at this site since around 1540 and is probably the earliest such church south of the equator.

16 March

Standing on the hilltop of Thompson's Hill, it is hard to imagine just what this island looked like before the arrival of man and goats.

What a lot of people do not realise is that at one time there were even wild hogs here. In March 1614, Thomas Best, commander of the English East India company's tenth voyage, left thirty of them in Lemon Valley in order to be able to guarantee fresh meat whenever a ship called at the island. This is recorded in papers left by a Cornish man named Peter Mundy. There were even domesticated horses here once, although I believe that there is now only one. Numerous donkeys make up for them.

With strong winds but hot sunshine, it was ideal weather for walking. So, during the afternoon, I set off heading for nowhere in particular and eventually found myself out at Barren Ground with no one about, a lone dog barking in a garden and birds singing all around me. I did find one or two purple granadillas, but I had expected to find a few more. It seems that they are now out of season.

As I looked across the sun-filled valleys and out to the glistening sea, I noticed that over towards High Peak the clouds were beginning to gather gradually, so I turned and made my way back, but as it turned out I had been a bit of a pessimist as even at midnight no rain had appeared.

17 March

Up before 6 a.m. this morning in order to carry about half a hundred weight of runner beans and pumpkins from the cottage to the tarmac road which must be about half a mile away. They are then to be transported by lorry to Jamestown market. This is one way in which some of the islanders supplement their income. In very slight drizzle, it was fresh enough not to be a chore.

With the weather still not really good enough during the morning to go on anything like a long walk, I busied myself with finding out about a few myths and legends about events on the island in yesteryear. Here are a few of them:

1. Friar's Rock, so named because once a Roman Catholic chapel stood in the valley and the friar fell in love with a local girl, who was a goatherd on nearby Goat Pound Ridge. They agreed to marry, but on the day of the wedding there was a fearful crack and the girl was swallowed up by the earth and the priest was turned to stone. It is not unreasonable to assume that neighbouring Crack Plain is where this occurred.

2. Black Oliver was a slave who on 5 May, 1673 guided three hundred and fifty British troops from a landing site on the rocks at Prosperous Bay, up to the cliffs to reach Jamestown by an 'impossible route'. In recognition of this, he was given his freedom and granted ownership of Walbro Hall, which is now in ruins, but lies below Teutonic Hall.

3. Billy Birch Cliff is so named because a lad of that name died by falling over it whilst driving his goats on 7 June, 1693.

4. Thompson's Valley is so named because it is a misspelling of Tomstone, a name used to describe the boulders lying in the valley (not tombstone).

5. Lemon Valley – named appropriately after the lemons that were introduced here in 1718.
6. At Gregory's Battery, a soldier committed suicide by throwing himself off the precipice and his so-called hand print is still there to be seen. This was in the late eighteenth century.
7. London's Ben. On the Barn, there once lived a hermit known only as London's Ben who had used to go missing whenever 'the white goat' called. This was often for considerable periods of time. Twenty years after he was last seen, in 1807, some men out shooting wild goats found some small caves that it is thought – judging by their contents – to have been his home.
8. In January, 1899, Bishop Welby was killed in a pony and trap accident on Shy Road. His ghost is still said to haunt the house where he lived at Oakbank. Just below is the bridge which is known, not unnaturally, as Bishop's Bridge.

During the afternoon, somewhere about three o'clock, the weather now being lovely and warm, it was off up the hill and out into the lanes. It is simply amazing how all these beautiful flowers seem to keep replacing each other on some sort of rota. No sooner does one plant die off than another one takes its place, even the prickly pear (tungi) are covered in pretty flowers. I think tomorrow I will go on a really long walk just to see what I might have missed to date, although I don't think that there can be too much. A whole day out, though, might just be the answer.

18 March

Retracing one's steps just to see what might have been missed first time around can be quite entertaining. Managed to get a lift to Silver Hill and from there walked to Pine Gate and then back to Silver Hill. It sounds simple enough. In actual fact the whole thing was probably about seven miles through incredible countryside, and every step well worth taking.

At Pine Gate the heavens opened and after buying some soft drinks to have at the picnic area at Green Hill, we took shelter on the porch of the clinic until the storm passed. Within twenty minutes the sun was shining so strongly that all trace of the storm was gone.

At Green Hill we had our soft drinks and sandwiches and a sit-down for thirty minutes or so before moving on. There is one garden as one leaves Green Hill that is full of pineapple plants; I had missed that last time around.

A couple of bends farther along the road, I was admiring some very pretty lantana flowers when a van pulled up and the driver inquired, 'Do you want to buy anything?'

I had no idea what he was selling until he opened the back of his van. It turned out he was the local travelling butcher. I think he was the only person we passed for several miles. Just after this, a very slight drizzle began to fall but this was to our advantage as it kept the temperature down without us getting too wet. In actual fact, I really think that we had missed hardly anything the first time around this area, but having said that it is a part of the island I would enjoy returning to again and again.

19 March

This was a day set aside for talking, and what a lot of talking we did. The subject was the industry of the island. Most of the work does tend to be done in the name of the St Helena government as with the police force, law courts, post office, Agriculture and Forestry Commission, education, medicine, road working, etc. or in the name of the island's largest employer, Solomon's.

Other than these obvious large employers, though, there are numerous diverse small firms or cottage industries ranging from fishermen to taxi drivers to hotel staff to shopkeepers, as well as a fish cannery, coffee bean growing, garden and horticultural nurseries, the market, and even cafés and bars. There are also private individuals who produce honey, candies, ice cream and such items to sell locally. Garden produce is also a source of income.

There was a fish cannery on the island in 1957 that was short-lived, but has now reopened and is very efficient and well-patronised. Few visitors leave for their homelands without a few tins of 'tuna from St Helena's sweet waters'.

The flax industry totally collapsed in December, 1957 after having been the island's principal employer for many decades. It was at its zenith in 1951 which, incidentally, was the only year in the history of St Helena when the income of the island exceeded its expenditure. The collapse was brought about by the introduction of synthetic fibres in place of the hemp used in the production of string. 1874 was the first year in which flax had been used commercially. At one time, 1,350 hectares were under cultivation, but now, in 1994, there is only flax that is wild and largely uncontrollable, probably about four hundred hectares at most. Most of the flax mills are now in ruins, although Woody Ridge, Broad Bottom and Bamboo Hedge do continue to be made use of, albeit for other reasons.

Some islanders find employment on the RMS *St Helena*, which is a far more reliable shipping line from the island's point of view than its predecessor the Union Castle Line, which, although paid huge subsidies to keep the UK–St Helena communication line open for passengers, left a lot to be desired as it suited them to gradually close it down. The RMS is owned by the Curnow Shipping Line of Helston, Cornwall.

20 March

We were invited out for the whole day by a family that live at Sappers Way. We were collected, fed, watered (the whisky wasn't) and entertained. We were made to feel so very welcome.

To those thinking of holidaying on the island, I would suggest that they endeavour to get themselves an invite of this sort as, believe me, the knowledge that they will pick up of St Helena and its ways can be quite a lot. The Saints are such easy-going people that they are genuine in everything that they say and do. I have heard them described as being 'nosy'. I believe what they really are is simply concerned – in my case anyway – that I was enjoying myself.

There is not a lot of money about on the island, but nevertheless not much is bought on credit. If they cannot afford it, then they don't get it until they can, and yet every home I have been into – and that is quite a number – are all very clean and reasonably furnished. The women all seem to be very house-proud, even in the remotest spots. As regards relating a scarcity of cash to having a good evening out at the weekend, it is worth pointing out that the discos are usually free to enter and many of the youngsters will probably settle for just one or two soft drinks all evening. Because of this, the halls fill up and they can all enjoy themselves, often for less than a pound a time.

I have before me a letter from Bishop Johnson who wrote to me when he knew I was coming to St Helena... 'The islanders are always ready to welcome visitors and I am sure you will find the island itself a most interesting place to explore and full of enchantment.'

I've found this to be totally correct. One bit of useless information I have gleaned is that both of the authors Robert Louis Stevenson and Jack London lived in St Helena. The catch is, though, that it was not this lovely island, but rather the winery town of the Napa Valley in California, USA.

21 March

I think we must be moving into the wet season now, as today it again rained heavily for most of the time. The clouds – fog, the Saints call them – were totally enveloping the whole of the south side of the island all day and I am told that even Jamestown spent almost all of it getting wet.

The uncertain climatic conditions at this time of the year does create problems for the local growers as both surplus and scarcity are totally unpredictable and many essential crops can well be ruined.

Here in Blue Hill one large area of fully formed green tomatoes have now been totally ruined by a form of blight, and I also know that many cucumbers over in Levelwood have succumbed. Fortunately the potatoes and other staple crops have survived; in fact they've done better than that, they've flourished.

Virtually all of the endemic trees prefer wet conditions, so that they are now really in their element, and the stands of plants such as marsh marigolds, arum lilies, ginger lilies and cannas can ask for nothing that they like better. The streams are looking really healthy along their banks and everywhere away from places of habitation the grass frogs can be heard calling.

One group that I did feel sorry for was the fairy terns, as, for the first time, I have seen them sitting on eggs, and the rain really must make these beautiful birds feel very uncomfortable. They do not look at ease on tree boughs at the best of times.

One plant that will appreciate all of this rain will be the small avenue of coconuts in Rupert's Bay. There have been several unsuccessful attempts to grow them commercially, most notably those introduced from India in 1731 by Governor Isaac Pyke, but all previous attempts have failed because the island's rainfall is too low. The present avenue was planted during the 1980s and to date appears to be successful.

Obviously, one group of people who will not altogether enjoy this poor weather will be the local fishermen, as the waves are not very friendly, to say the least.

22 March

Rain again all morning. Quite heavy, although it was reasonably warm.

Today I was informed by telephone that the school children in England had received their pen-pal letters from their counterparts here on the island. That is pleasing to know. I hope some may lead to lifelong friendships.

Afternoon saw us walking to Cason's and on round the first road on our right, which leads ultimately to either Sandy Bay or Hutt's Gate, depending on one's choice. Along this road are some lovely plants, especially the large sweet-scented ladies' petticoats (moon flowers), with their white eight-inch trumpets draping down like festoons and surrounded by yellow everlasting flowers, fuchsias, wild ginger lilies with their heady scent, a few St John's lilies, and an assortment of smaller flowers such as lantana in a mixture of colours. This was far enough for today, so we retraced our steps, but on almost reaching High Peak we did halt awhile to watch some workers who were cutting down some kaffir booms (thorn trees). At this point the sun did manage to get through for a while. It was very welcome.

The fields around really looked green and healthy after all the rain; in fact every growing thing looked to be in perfect condition. We went on past High Peak that also looked very tempting, but we didn't really fancy tackling it there and then due to the possibility of mud right at the summit. Geologically, High Peak is, to put it mildly, of no special interest at all, because it is merely a slightly more resistant to erosion rock than that which forms the main volcanic shield. However, many endemic plants flourish here.

23 March

Decided to find out today about one or two of the better known wrecks that lie at the bottom of James Bay. I have already referred to the *Witte Leeuw* in 1613. Apparently, there are several Dutch and Portuguese ships dating back to the seventeenth century, but in actual fact only three have left any tangible legacy: firstly the *Witte Leeuw* and its porcelain cargo; then the *Papanui* which sank in flames in 1911, and whose steering gear is still clearly visible and is marked by a light at night-time; and of course HMS *Darkdale*. This was an auxiliary oil tanker that was torpedoed under cover of darkness by a German U-boat in 1941. The hull still lies on the sea floor and still occasionally leaks oil when it moves in storms – well over fifty years later.

It is of interest to note that the German battleship *Graf Spee* appeared off Jamestown on her final voyage, when she retreated to the River Plate. The sinking of the *Darkdale* was the only actual action on or around the island in terms of battle.

Another ship lost, although not in James Bay, was the *Waterwitch*. She was a Royal Navy sloop that was lost at sea whilst chasing slaving ships. There is a well-merited monument to her in the public gardens recalling St Helena's part in the fight against slavery. For those who do not know, emancipation was brought about by the British Government in 1832, but the Royal Navy had to bring a lot of pressure to bear on the slaving ships. Many an unrecorded British sailor lost his life in the process – take the *Waterwitch* as an example.

Whilst on the subject of slavery, another fact that I have uncovered is that probably most slaves were brought from Madagascar. In fact, as long ago as 1717, a quarantine station was set up in Lemon Valley for them because so many of them were infected with smallpox. The same station was last used to accommodate Boer prisoners who had come into contact with bubonic plague in Cape Town.

The sunshine returned to us at about 2.50 p.m. so it was utilised by going on to the garden and collecting about twenty pounds of runner beans and fifteen large cucumbers along with some bilberries to take to the vegetable market in Jamestown tomorrow morning. In doing this, we unsettled a small flock of waxbills that I had not even realised were there, they are so small. These tiny birds live almost exclusively on hay grass seeds, and I do fear for their future as kikuyu grass begins to dominate.

24 March

Up and away by 7 a.m. in order to get the cucumbers and beans to the market in Jamestown. A full day down in Jamestown is always interesting and this was no exception. We went around the various monuments and these are what we found:

In the centre of Grand Parade is one that reads:

> This monument was erected by the inhabitants of St Helena and friends overseas to the memory of the Hon WJJ Arnold CMB MB DPH born 22 April, 1867 at Belfast died 29 January, 1925 whilst administering the government of this colony. Colonial surgeon from 1903 to 1925. Served during the Great War and was the greatest friend that St Helena ever had.

Opposite to this monument is the library which has two plaques on its outside front wall, one reads:

> In memory of the nine persons killed by the fall of 1,500 tons of rock 17 April, 1890.

And the other one reads:

> This tablet is erected by the 364 passengers in appreciation of the kindness and hospitality shown to them by the inhabitants of this island 11 September–14 October, 1911.

This latter refers to the loss of the *Papanui*.

In the public gardens is a column erected to the memory of many of the crew of the *Waterwitch* who lost their lives whilst stamping out slavery. This sloop/brig was of course lost herself eventually. This column reads:

> This column was erected by the commander, officers and crew of Her Majesty's brig *Waterwitch* to the memory of their shipmates

who died while serving on the coast of Africa AD 1839–1843. The greater number died while absent in captured slave vessels. Their remains were either left in different parts of Africa or given to the sea. The graves alike are all undistinguished. This island is selected for the record because three lie buried here and because the deceased, as well as their surviving comrades, ever met the warmest welcome from its inhabitants.

The other three sides of this column are filled with the details of these lost sailors. I have simply listed a couple of them in order to give some idea of the facts.

Samuel Knight, marine drowned in an attempt to board a slave vessel 10 February, 1842, aged twenty-four years.
William Plant, boatswain's mate. Died in England on his return journey from the United States 1 February, 1841, aged forty-two years.
Thomas Gibbs, ord. Died at sea 10 October, 1839, aged twenty-four years.

Over the wharf is the war memorial which simply reads, 'The glorious dead 1914–18, 1939–45'.

Crossing the bridge from the wharf into town, one passes an archway which bears the coat of arms of the East India Company but on its other (town) side is a line marking the flood level on 14 April, 1878. That must have been colossal. There is a lot of history here, both told and untold. There is also the clock outside the market that is dedicated to the men who lost their lives in the 1914–18 conflict.

25 March

A gentle breeze and early morning sunshine augured well for the day. We are now moving into autumn in the southern hemisphere, and I see that the dahlias that grow all along one side of the garden are just beginning to die off. This is compensated for by thick bushes of honeysuckle and ever more everlasting flowers (yellow helichrysum) and geraniums, all of which grow wild and uncultivated here.

There is one area of erosion on this island called the Artist's Palette because of the colours there. I believe that name could be applied to the whole place. If you can show me a writer or a painter who is tired of St Helena then I'll show you a person who is tired of life.

We decided to go into town in the early afternoon to see the arrival of the RMS *St Helena* from the UK. This was due at 3 p.m. so we needed to be in Jamestown before that in order to avoid the traffic coming in from the outlying villages, as on a 'boat day' almost everyone has someone to meet or at least some eagerly awaited mail to collect. The delivery system is not quite as comprehensive as in England. Then again, this is all part of the excitement of island life.

Where the larger boats and ships anchor is well out in the bay at seventeen fathoms where they are safe from the rollers which did – way back in 1846 – wreck the wharf. The existing wharf dates from 1914.

After having been down to the wharf ourselves, and having mixed with many people that we have already made friends with, we moved on up the Main Street into the town where we were being treated to a lovely three-course meal by a family of special friends from Levelwood who could not have looked after us better if we had been royalty. This is an island of real friendship, it really is. After the meal we took a stroll along the wharf to look at the RMS *St Helena* riding out in the anchorage with all her lights ablaze – a really lovely sight.

26 March

The weather today was of two extremes; torrential rain all morning and blazing hot sunshine all afternoon. Saw some red cardinals (malagasy fody) ripping some flowers to pieces in their search for insects. In fairness to them, they were wild flowers.

There seemed to be an extra large number of butterflies and bees around, and there were also quite a lot of moths. Other than these, we found quite a number of blushing snails that the rain had brought out. We also had a bit of a scout around to try to find the elusive St Helena earwig, but needless to say we again came up with a blank.

Early evening we decided to go into Jamestown again – the third time in as many days – and took a walk from the wharf round to Ladder Hill Point and saw there a most spectacular bird about the size of a herring gull, white with some black bars on the wings and a vicious looking beak. The tail feathers were elongated. It was the bird the Saints call the tropy bird (tropic bird). They were obviously returning from a day's fishing, although I am told you are quite likely to find one or two round in Breakneck Valley at any time of the day. It seems that there is a small congregation of them that live there.

As darkness moved in, the lights of the RMS again dominated the scene at the wharf steps, and it was time to retire to the Consulate for a few nightcaps before going back to Blue Hill.

27 March

The warmth of last evening was suspended for a while this morning as so much rain fell for an hour or so it was like being in a bath. The variations in the weather of the island all add to its excitement and beauty. As the clouds (steam) cleared, they left a really clear view of the surrounding countryside and the inlets to the sea down in the valley, and looking to the peaks above, the whole vista created a never-to-be-forgotten scenario.

One thing that did occur during the early afternoon was that the RMS departed from the anchorage, bound for Ascension Island. At about the same time, the church that covers Silver Hill and Levelwood was putting on a special service that drew a very large congregation of worshippers whose Sunday best clothing was fit to bedeck the finest families anywhere I have ever been. With the scarcity of money on the island, it left me absolutely dumbstruck. I was looking at dresses that would in all probability cost over one hundred pounds each worn by girls and ladies whose whole family income could not exceed forty pounds weekly. Each man and boy wore a well-tailored suit. They must go without quite a lot to afford such clothes.

About 5 p.m., we passed another small group of these well-dressed worshippers at Woody Ridge. I assume that they had been to the same service.

As a point of interest, Woody Ridge is one of only four flax mills that is still utilised. Although Fairyland flax mill is the only one – and only occasionally – used for its original purpose, Woody Ridge is used as a base for Solomon's farming activities. Quite a number of pheasants were to be seen here again, and also a few rabbits.

On then to Hutt's Gate which appeared to be deserted, and then Whitegate where evensong was about to start. Cason's, High Peak and Thompson's Hill rounded off a very full day.

28 March

The *QEII* liner was due in this morning, but has already fallen one day behind on her round-the-world schedule and so will not be in until tomorrow morning at six o'clock. Think about it – if this, undoubtedly the premier passenger liner in the world can be out in her timing, what must the situation have been like in the sixteenth and seventeenth centuries before St Helena was settled in by the English? There is a so-called 'post stone' just outside the castle where certainly the Dolphin, and probably many more ships, used to leave their mail to be picked up by the next one travelling in the right direction.

Mention of the castle does bring me to a point of interest. It was used as the governor's residence until the middle of the nineteenth century. Having been released from its military use with the construction of the fort, for over three hundred years the offices of the St Helena government have been housed there.

Of interest also is the Consulate Hotel. About a hundred years ago it was called the Royal Hotel but eventually its name was altered in recognition of it having been the American consulate from 1847. Nearby are the Canister and the very important-looking Victorian Malabar Store, which is now used by Solomon's as a warehouse.

One geological area that intrigued me as to how it got its name is just around the corner from Ladder Hill Point and known as Breakneck Valley. Now I know. It dates back to the early days when sailors reported that they were likely to break their hearts climbing up the hills and break their necks coming down them.

Way back in 1708, a certain Captain Mashbone caused considerable excitement, which was actually encouraged by Governor Roberts, when he reported that he had found both gold and silver in Breakneck Valley. On having these minerals assayed in England they were found to be only iron pyrites. The only form of semi-precious stone that appears to have been successfully mined here was at the Cornelian mine, excavated on the instructions of Governor Beatson in the early 1800s. The hole is now largely refilled and is to be found at Turks Cap Valley.

There is so much of interest throughout this island I think a whole series of books could be written, given the opportunity.

Knowing that we have a long day ahead of us, the walking had been kept to a minimum and an early night taken.

29 March

On the way into Jamestown this morning, we saw a baby donkey that could not have been a week old lying with its mother in a field near the turn off to Fairyland. It really did look a picture.

At 8 a.m., we departed for the wharf at Jamestown so that we could video film the *QEII* at the anchorage. She had arrived there at 6 a.m. and was leaving at 1 p.m. I don't think just seven hours is really enough time for her passengers to actually realise that they have been to this island, although it is adequate for us to get our footage of film. With upwards of 2,000 people being added to the 5,500 Saints, the whole island did seem to be rather overcrowded. A particularly nice first day cover envelope and postage stamp was issued to celebrate the visit of the ship to the island, and fortunately the weather was fine. All the bars and hotels opened at 9 a.m. and they did a good trade, as did the taxi and hire car drivers.

Having spent the day in town we went to an art exhibition in the evening that was held at the Consulate Hotel. Everyone of note on the island seemed to be there, ranging from the governor and his wife through to just about every tradesman.

Of interest is the fact that the *QEII* is the second largest passenger liner in the world, and she is also the fastest.

30 March

Last night the moonlight was so strong and the sky so clear – not a cloud in sight, only numerous stars – that I decided to find out about the astronomical activity of Edmund Halley who had an observatory built just above Hutt's Gate at a spot that is now called Halley's Mount. Halley visited St Helena from February 1677 to March 1678 to continue with his work of making a chart of the stars of the southern hemisphere that would link up with one of the northern hemisphere. He had considered that St Helena would be an ideal spot for this task, but it was only after he had established his observatory that he realised that he had selected one of the cloudiest places on earth. Regardless of this though, he was still able to achieve one fantastic feat in that he succeeded in establishing the distance between the earth and the sun by using figures based on the transit of the planet Mercury. He further recommended that these figures should be cross-checked by using the transit of Venus in a further eighty-four years time. This was done by the astronomer Neville Maskelyne in 1761 who had build an extension of Halley's Mount Ridge to perform this feat. The figures matched.

Unfortunately, there is nothing left to see of the extension. The remains of Halley's observatory were rediscovered in 1970 and excavated. Still on this type of subject, just across on the hill opposite is the site of St Helena's first meteorological station that was built in 1892.

Each of these places is well signposted at a bend in the road at Hutt's Gate.

During the afternoon we went out to Donkey Plain where we saw the bones of many sea birds. I am told they are also to be seen at Sugar Loaf, Dry Gut, Sandy Bay and Prosperous Bay. They are the remains of sea bird colonies that existed up to the time of the island's discovery and the introduction of cats. Apparently the principal breeds of bird at that time would have been burrow-nesting petrels and shearwaters. Now, other than the fairy terns, the only sea birds now on St Helena are those that nest high in the cliffs.

Weather-wise, the day was perfect, with some wind but really strong sunshine and only very little cloud, but I am told that during the evening that there was thunder and lightning at Half Tree Hollow for the first time in years.

31 March

Maundy Thursday. Traditionally, this is the best night of the year for fishermen here on St Helena. I know of some who went to Rupert's Bay for that very purpose. I was not among them.

At about 10 a.m., we went into Jamestown in order to go to the treasury but as it did not open for a further hour, decided to walk up to Munden's Battery which is an interesting walk as at all times we could see the panoramic view of the wharf and harbour as well as across the town to Jacob's Ladder. We looked down on a derelict house where the island housed its last political prisoners from 1957 to 1961 – three Bahreini princes. All along this walk, at regular intervals along the rock face, are metal rings which were placed there in order to assist in the handling of the exceptionally heavy guns that were placed at the upper Munden's Battery.

Back down in Jamestown, business was concluded and after a pleasant meal we decided to walk up Side Path out of town and on to Levelwood via Longwood, Hutt's Gate and Silver Hill. What a walk that was. We called in at Hutt's Gate church and signed the visitor's book, but sadly it appeared to me that this church is being allowed to run down a little. We then walked on in perfect weather as far as Alarm Hill at which point we left the beaten track for a little while and sat down and relaxed. There are numerous young fir trees planted in this area and it really is a beautiful place. Suitably refreshed, it was then on to Levelwood forest where there were numerous baby waxwings to disturb underfoot and the calling of frogs was incessant. There are wild pumpkins growing here as well as lovely ripe red raspberries and blackberries and also paw-paws. The eucalyptus trees have pride of place along most of the ridges in the forest.

Emerging at Silver Hill it was a gradual descent into Levelwood and the walk had been successfully concluded. It had taken all of four hours, but what a walk. As I do keep saying, the scenery on this island is absolutely unbeatable.

Referring back to Munden's I am told it is an excellent point to see skuas that have migrated south for the winter. I must confess that I did look for them, but unfortunately did not see any.

1 April

The RMS is in, having brought workers home from both Ascension and the Falkland islands, some for good and some on leave. The town, I am told, is full so it is a good day to keep out of it I would think, especially as it is a bank holiday, Good Friday, with all the shops shut and just the bars and hotels open. After all of yesterday's walking, the legs can do with a rest anyway.

Knowing that I would be in all day, I decided to look up any odd facts that I could find about various governors of St Helena. Here are a few:

1. Governor Blackmore fell from his horse and was killed in 1691 on a path that no longer exists near Heart-Shaped Waterfall.

2. Governor Beatson was the man in the 1800s who gave the instructions for the go-ahead of the Cornelian mine.

3. Governor Patton had the Sister's Walk promenade below Munden's built during his period of office (1802–1807).

4. Governor Sir John Field, a far more recent holder of office, from 1962–1968 had Field Road, which leads off Side Road, named after him.

5. Governor Hudson Ralph Janisch. The only 'Saint' ever to have become the governor – in the mid-nineteenth century – is buried at Knollcombes.

6. Governor Sir Hudson J Lowe was the man in office at the time of Napoleon Bonaparte's death. To put it mildly, he was not a fervent admirer of the defeated French emperor.

7. Governor Jenkins was the man who had the War of Jenkins Ear named after him in which the English gave the

Spanish 'a fearful hiding'. He was in office from 1740–1742.

8. Governor Lambert, whom I have referred to previously was the man who, in 1742, rushed the building of the fortifications at Sandy Bay by deciding not to use mortar, so causing a rapid deterioration of them.

9. Governor Captain Roberts was the one who, in 1708, urged Captain Mashbone to send samples of supposed gold and silver to be assayed in England. It turned out to be only iron pyrites.

10. Governor Peel was the last governor to die on the island. The pavilion on Francis Plain was built in 1925 to honour him.

11. Governor Massingham in 1984 took a ducking at the steps to the wharf while helping Prince Andrew ashore (probably a good one to mention on April Fool's Day).

12. Governor Isaac Pyke in 1731 introduced coconuts from India, along with coffee and maize.

In the late afternoon I took a walk to West Lodge in the pleasant sunshine, but found the gates were wired up to make sure the cattle didn't roam away. This certainly was a minus mark on this walk, even if understandable.

2 April

The answers to the pen-pal letters are now beginning to be received by the St Helena children and they are quite excited. It is nice to see.

I saw that both at Blue Hill school and in Thompson's Wood there were lots of tents pitched as families are camping out for the Easter weekend. A number of youngsters were doing the same thing down on Sandy Bay beach. The night of Good Friday was windy and wet, but this morning, with the sun shining, it really did look like successful camping weather. Thompson's Wood is probably the Saints' favourite camping ground and is used in January for the Jamestown Scouts' annual camp. They certainly enjoy life here.

There was one plant growing in a large patch near Cabbage Tree Road that I could not identify. I took a sprig of it to find out the answer and was told that it was jellico. It had no flowers, but that is not surprising as it usually flowers in December. Apparently it was once used as a substitute for angelica, as a result of which it got its present name.

In the same area I also found some dogwood trees, easily recognised by their dark green elongated leaves with prominent veins. Here again, the flowers were out of season although I am told they are small and greenish white and appear in clusters at the end of stems. The other endemic plants found here were all of the cabbage trees, black, she and he, and of course the tree fern.

For anyone visiting the island who is interested in this subject this is the local spot to visit, but whatever else you do, do not forget that you will require good walking boots as this walk will take you on up to the peaks, and the way is well overgrown in many places, mainly with flax. Having said that though, you do get some magnificent views. At this point is an area with the pleasing name of Newfoundland, and it is a name generally applied to the southern edge of the peaks. How it actually got its name I admit I have failed to ascertain, but I will. I have tried to find out through local enquiries to no avail.

3 April

Easter Sunday: covered quite a large number of miles today. Set off at about 8.30 a.m. and did not see a single soul until we got to the gates to the arboretum and that was just the man who checks on the cattle. On then to Whitegate and Hutt's Gate, calling in between at Knollcombes to see the Baptist chapel where the Boer prisoners who died from various diseases are buried.

The house standing nearby was at one time owned by a man named Brigadier General Pine Coffin. He was garrison commander way back in 1823. Black Gate, Silver Hill and Levelwood, followed by Alice's Point and Rock Rose and back to Levelwood for dinner and tea before driving home, saw out the day.

At several points it was obvious that the lovely wild ginger lilies were still the principal flowers around, although, especially at the junction of Cabbage Tree Road, the lace plant is now coming into fashion more and more. Flax is everywhere on this journey, as is gorse. Hibiscus and freesias are in profusion as is nasturtium along the roadside. Near the water tank that stands nearer to Alice's Point than any other feature I can name, we found the one black spot of the walk – thousands of tiny little thunderflies and we got covered in them. The incident was all over in minutes though, and the continuation of the walk was pleasant.

I know it was Easter Sunday so that everything could be expected to be quiet, but we saw only one vehicle between Silver Hill and Rock Rose for the complete return journey. In such lovely countryside, this is ideal for walking, looking and listening.

4 April

Easter Monday. Virtually the whole island is picnicking.

Walked up to Thompson's Wood then to a vantage position to video some of Sandy Bay beach, Rock Rose, The Peaks, Lot and Lot's Wife and Green Hill – all from the Cason's to Blue Hill Road near Thompson's Hill. On then to see the Seychelles tortoises at Plantation House; then to New Ground, Half Tree Hollow and down to the top of Ladder Hill where we went to study the two very large guns and their emplacements together with batteries, ammunition stores and sleeping quarters. This is a very interesting site.

Then down Ladder Hill into Jamestown and so to the wharf where we enjoyed both food and drink before going round Ladder Hill Point to look again at the trophy birds swooping around the cliffs of Breakneck Valley. There were quite a lot of them here this time. A little light-hearted fishing was entered into and one silverfish and two small old wives were caught but returned to the sea.

The whole time that we were there, the waves were really pounding the sea wall and rocks, and for most of the time it was really hot. There is a sign below where the trophy birds are based that warns that the area has been designated dangerous due to rock falls. As we looked again, closer, at the cliff walls it is surprising just how many fairy terns and rock pigeons are nesting on small crevices there. Returning through Jamestown the overriding noise near to the market is the babble of the mynah birds; that really is a loud chatter. It was then a race to get back to Blue Hill before darkness closed in.

5 April

I spent a large proportion of today searching through records trying to find out how certain places had acquired their names. These are some of them, although I am still struggling to find out about Newfoundland:

13. Bencoolen – named after a town in Sumatra, an East India company post.
14. Cavalho Hole – named after the cavalley fish, a type of jack.
15. Chubb's Rock – named after Edward Chubb who fell to his death in 1683.
16. Cockburn's Battery – named after the admiral who escorted Napoleon into exile.
17. Coles' Rock – John Coles was murdered by a slave named Sultan in 1721 by being throttled.
18. Cooks Bridge – named after the supervisor who constructed it in late 1960s.
19. Cowpath – a pathway leading up the cliff at Half Tree Hollow constructed to enable cattle to be moved quickly should there be a threat from unrecognised ships.
20. Deadwood – named after the area lost as a result of ravages from goats when they roamed the Great Wood. In 1720 a stone wall was built to stop this occurring but neither the wall nor interest in its cause were continued.
21. French's Gut – named in the eighteenth century after a gunner John French.
22. Hancock's Hole – Richard Hancock, a member of the gang known as the Dennison Rebellion Mutineers, who

murdered the governor in 1684. He was a fugitive hiding in this hole for twenty-two months.

23. Head O'Wain – from head of vein, a geological feature.

24. Iron Pot – named after the large try house that whalers used for boiling blubber during the nineteenth century.

25. Ladder Hill – dates back to 1680 and refers to a rope ladder used to scale it, almost two hundred years before the present ladder was constructed in the form it is now.

26. Manati Bay – named after what were originally considered to be manatees or sea cows. They were wiped out by commercial sealers, and consequently none had been sighted off St Helena since 1819.

27. Mount Ross – takes its name from Governor Sir Patrick Ross (1846–50).

28. Oaklands Hotel – built during the eighteenth century, it was so named as it was then surrounded by oak trees. There are none left there now.

29. Old Lufkins and Lufkins Spring – although well apart, these take their titles from John Lufkin who was captured by the Dennison mutineers of 1684. He had a chequered future then, firstly being accused of conspiracy, but then being pardoned (not acquitted).

30. Piccolo Hill – received this name as it was the call sign for the DWS aerial complex monitoring most West Africa communications and satellites.

31. Pine Path – the route of a pipe taking water from a desalinisation plant from Ruperts to Boer prisoners on Deadwood Plain.

32. Powell's Valley – Gabriel Powell was an early settler in 1673.

33. Rupert's Bay – probably named after Prince Rupert of English Civil War fame, as it is known he called here on his return from India.

34. Shark Valley – called this after the mackerel sharks hereabouts.

35. The Barnes Road – Major Barnes supervised the prisoners and freed slaves, in about the 1850s, in the building of the road.

36. Wrangham's – this was simply the eighteenth century home of the Wrangham family.

6 April

I had a letter from England today dated 22 February, 1994. It had taken forty-three days.

With the boat arriving once every two months, I suppose that that is not so surprising really. This island really is remote, but that is part of its undoubted charm and attraction.

The sunshine was lovely and warm and I have simply run out of superlatives to describe both the flowers and the trees. On top of these facts the bird life was doing its best to make us welcome, with the turtle doves coo-cooing, the mynah birds squawking and quarrelling and the Swainson's canaries going into full song. I do wonder whether I am still on earth or in paradise. Even the hens with their week-old chicks add to this feeling.

7 April

To some extent this was a rerun of Easter Monday, especially with regards to the video filming because most of that day's film had not been successful. This time was okay. We used two different points from which to film Sandy Bay and we also filmed Man and Horse pastures.

What I saw first thing this morning that impressed me in these surroundings was that as I walked up the road alongside West Lodge, five pheasants suddenly took fright and flew right across me. I'd never seen more than two together here before.

I spent about twenty minutes or more talking to the road workers out at Blue Hill and found them to be very sociable, friendly people – well, everyone here is anyway. They have to work three days a week on clearing the roads and edges if they are unemployed in order to get just £24 a week. Can you imagine this happening in England?

We had dinner in Jamestown and did more video filming there, especially around the wharf and swimming pool area, and then returned to base to confirm it was all right this time. It was. We had been very fortunate with the weather. Although it was very windy, especially around the ridges of Sandy Bay, the sun shone all day long. One spot that caught the imagination was Thompson's Wood – Botley's Road below Ball Alley. We will go there tomorrow.

One point of real interest today was when we called at the shop at St Paul's and then visited the churchyard there. As we walked in, all of the first batch of graves on the left-hand side were for military personnel. There was even one for a member of the St Helena Home Guard.

8 April

Another day in which we walked many miles. We retraced the steps taken on 19 February, but with a little more added on.

The wind blowing directly down Ball Alley was howling as it usually does, but the views from there of Man and Horse, Speery Island and the Gates of Chaos were marvellous, as indeed were those of Sandy Bay and its surroundings when we turned around. Many very good photographs were taken here and hereabouts. We went on to Distant Cottage which is now uninhabited and then to Horse Ridge below Hooper's Ridge to the WWF reserve where immediately outside the dilapidated ruin of a house were quite a number of young ebony trees all bearing lovely pure white flowers.

The ruined house was known by two different names, both correct. They were Horse Riding Hill House and White's. Next was another ruin called Old Lufkins. Then up and up through the flax to eventually reach the road at the end of Hooper's Ridge, having stopped and had a picnic on the pathway through the flax. It was then all downhill back to Blue Hill village. Later in the day, between Cason's and Pine Gate we saw a lovely cluster of arum lilies, undoubtedly the largest number I have seen of them at one time.

The whole area around the lanes of the island is now aflame with colour from multitudes of flowers. There seem to be more by the day now and there were plenty to start with. We were flown over by a flock of about two hundred Java sparrows near Green Hill and that was a sight worth seeing as well. My only problem here is taking it all in.

9 April

On Hooper's Ridge above Old Lufkins I saw an old picket house and the magazine when I was there yesterday. This fuelled my interest so I decided to devote today to old military batteries and paraphernalia.

Firstly come the lower and upper Munden batteries in Jamestown and then, along the top of Rupert's Ridge are Saddle and Sampson's batteries. Probably the most perfectly preserved guns on the island are the Sampson's cannons. Also at Rupert's Bay, but in the valley this time, are the remains of a fortified line that was the longest one on the island, built and continually improved during the eighteenth century. Banks battery is really a conglomeration of fortifications that must have been highly specialised in their day, strategically positioned to look over the roads to spot any sailing ship approaching.

The first recorded fortification here was in 1678 and the name Banks was that of the officer in charge of that early building. This was later rebuilt. The cannons are still lying there to this day. The slots of a portcullis are visible. Before that the King William's Fort was built, it becoming the main battery which now lies below, submerged in water.

On again, following a track from Half Moon are three more batteries, named Repulse Point, Middle Point and Turk's Cap where stand the Cox's and Gregory's batteries, strategically placed to overlook Prosperous Bay, whilst the Dutch battery overlooks Turk's Cap Bay.

Powell's battery overlooks Powell's Bay and is situated a little way back up the Powell Valley, and Crown Point battery stands on the coast at Potato Bay approaching Sandy Bay beach and overlooking the landing place at Horse's Head. Fallen from the cliff above is a pair of cannons that appear to be early or mid-eighteenth century vintage and are embedded and almost totally buried in black sand and earth on the old parade ground of Sandy Bay beach. There is also a couple of magazines here.

Fortifications are also situated at Seale's battery and at Horse's Head itself. This is where Governor Lambert built his ill-fated defence wall in 1742. There is the Eagle's Eyrie battery and another fortification alongside it at the junction of Water Gut with Thompson's Bay and an unnamed battery overlooking Thompson's Valley island. Combined, these batteries would appear the most formidable to any would-be attacker on the whole of the island.

There is a further battery on Friar's Ridge overlooking Lemon Valley fort and the old disused quarantine station, and another one at Goat Pound Ridge. Of more recent times, but still outdated, are the two heavy gun emplacements, quarters and stores situated at the top of Ladder Hill. These guns have been fired – if only for practice – within living memory.

There is also an old disused gun battery across from the Baptist chapel in Sandy Bay, and of course there is High Knoll Fort. With the island so comprehensively defended, it is little wonder that it was never attacked, other than the 1673 invasion by the Dutch which was short-lived.

10 April

Having dealt with military historical features yesterday, I went for natural geological features today and did a study of the various guts on the island. Guts are streams discharging into valleys rather than into the sea directly. One gut – Broad Gut – is the exception to the rule. I managed to locate seventeen named guts and they are:

37. Bilberry Field Gut – this is at Bottoms Wood.

38. Broad Gut – at Sandy Bay right down to the beach. It is well marked out in its upper reaches by a beautiful green finger of plants.

39. Dry Gut – Woody Ridge to Bencoolen.

40. French's Gut – borehole near High Peak.

41. Hunt's Gut – near Halley's mount.

42. Lemon Tree Gut – near Manati Bay from Wild Ram Spring.

43. Mulberry Gut – near to Longwood farm.

44. Netley Gut – this is on Deadwood Plain.

45. Peak Gut – near to Bouncer's Ridge and Peak Dale farm.

46. Perkins Gut – from near the Bamboo Grove to Wrangham's.

47. Potato Gut – at Potato Bay.

48. Retreat Gut – at Barren Hill.

49. Salt Gut – this meanders a lot and is at Partridge Rock and Devil's Garden.

50. Swampy Gut – this is from Brown's Hill to Stitche's Ridge.

51. Warren's Gut – this is below Alarm Hill and basically runs from Jimmy Lot's Spring to the waterfall and beyond.

52. Wash House Gut – this is below the ridges from Long Ground Ridge to Sheep Knoll.

53. Water Gut – near Man and Horse pastures and has a sheep pound in it.

On the debit side today, I have effectively spoiled two complete rolls of film which I do not think I will have time to replace as so much travelling was involved in taking them. Never mind, though; I do have some others completed successfully.

As one travels around the periphery of the island, it appears that there are just twenty-eight small islets scattered around it. Fifteen are so small that they are not named, but the thirteen larger ones are known as Rough Rock Island, Flat Rock Island, Sandy Bay Island, Egg Island, Black Horse Island, Long Cove, Old Father Point Island, Speery Island, Black Rock, Thompson's Valley Island, Shore Island, George Island and of course the Chimney, which is a pillar of rock off Nigger's Head. The largest, by far, of these twenty-eight islands are Speery Island and Egg Island.

Egg Island is connected to the mainland of St Helena by rocks just below the surface known as a tombolo, and I am told that in the Twenties this tombolo was above sea level. Something must be moving.

11 April

Found two more guts today: Woodlands Gut, which basically connects Myrtle Farm to Broad Bottom Mill Farm and Briars Gut, which is from near the Briars Pavilion to East Lodge.

I also found a couple of boreholes, one in French's Gut and the other at Iron Pot, which is between Little Broad Bottom and Goldinine Gate. The scenery everywhere around these areas is unbelievably beautiful. What I do find remarkable is that a large proportion of Saints do not know where some of these places are, bearing in mind the smallness of this island. I've still not found out yet how Newfoundland got its name.

During the afternoon we walked towards George Island via the Taglate Valley, Lazy Point and Bencoolen, but because of the extreme heat at this low altitude, we turned back just short of Hancock's Hole. The scenery here, mainly brought about because of erosion, is breathtaking. With both Little Stone Top and Great Stone Top looking down on us, it was quite different to anywhere else I have ever been, even on St Helena.

Amazingly amongst all this erosion we saw a small shrew. It obviously was able to find something to live on.

There is talk of building an airport on St Helena – in fact there has been for years – and the proposed site is on Prosperous Plain which is right alongside Bencoolen and the Taglate Valley. What a vision that would make for the plane's passengers with the Sandy Bay panorama as well just around the corner, as it were. The initial flood of brochures would be the most sought after in the world if accompanied with well-taken photographs from the air.

Just to round things off on a different note, returning late at night to Blue Hill we had a flat tyre. So in total darkness we had to change the wheel at the lane-side on a very winding stretch of lane. Isn't it always the way?

12 April

Had to go into Jamestown today to get our immigration permits renewed as they initially cover only three calendar months and we will exceed that period slightly.

Going down Ladder Hill I noticed quite a number of infant trees, sprung from bird droppings or wind-blown seeds. They probably will not survive on this rocky slope, but at least they are trying.

Business completed, we went to Half Tree Hollow and looked around the part of it that is called Cow Path. There are some really nice houses there with some fantastic views both out over the Atlantic Ocean and also over Jamestown's valley towards the Briars and Longwood. A very nice spot.

After this we drove – not walked – back into Jamestown, then up Side Path and on to Longwood and Hutt's Gate, Silver Hill, Levelwood, Windy Ridge, where we met a man in a van who had run out of petrol. Hutt's Gate again to tell his wife, then to Whitegate, Cason's and so to Blue Hill. Rather a lot of miles through flower-bedecked lanes, to say nothing of the con tours of the hills and valleys. It really is a mouth-watering island. I don't think I could live in a city or a large town ever again after this experience.

13 April

It had been arranged that we would go fishing during the night, but the signs were bad so it was cancelled, which was just as well as several short, sharp squalls occurred. By 7.30 a.m., though, the sun was shining and the day became very hot.

There is a high long hill to the right of Little and Great Stone Tops looking from Windy Ridge that is simply called Boxwood. This and Long Range are the only two recorded places where the Boxwood shrub are listed as having been seen for a hundred years or so. This shrub is up to two metres in height with small, greyish leaves and single white flowers under the foliage.

I looked and I looked, as I did a few weeks ago for the St Helena earwig, but I could not find one. I suppose that both are really extinct, but somehow I get the feeling that with so much of the island largely untrodden it could just be possible to find one or the other tucked away somewhere. Let's face it, the ebony had been written off for a hundred years prior to being rediscovered in November 1980. There are now several thousand cuttings and trees around St Helena. Wouldn't it be marvellous to find one?

I spent the whole of the late afternoon and early evening talking to an elderly lady who was interested in black magic, voodoo and spirits. I promised not to tell anything of what she told me and I will adhere to that. It is quite frightening if true, and a few people here do believe in it. Who am I to say that they are wrong? It is certainly not something to meddle with.

14 April

This was a blistering hot day all over the island. At about 1.30 p.m., I was invited on a tour of St Paul's School on Francis Plain, and found it to be of a much better standard than I had expected. The science laboratories were quite exceptional, as were the practical facilities for woodwork, building and motor mechanics. These are the subjects I was impressed with but in actual fact it appeared that every classroom on the ground was very proficiently used. The subject being taught in the history class was the Korean war. How is that for teaching an unlikely subject to island schoolchildren? It certainly gives them a broader view on the world.

Later on I went to the public library to see if they could assist me further in my search for the origin of the name Newfoundland. They could not, but I looked through one or two reference books dealing with the island and came across an Ordnance that stated that any Negro or Negroes who stole anything worth eighteen pence would have twenty lashes of the whip administered by his master! It seems unbelievable in this day and age that those times existed.

As I came back past the Market Hall, I saw that they were selling chow-chows at twenty pence each. I have seen many of these growing wild at Levelwood forest. They are vegetables that look something like misformed marrows and are used like potatoes.

Having come past Whitegate, I saw the hedgerows are now awash with the heavily-scented Whitewood, which has all come into flower at once, interlaced with lovely blue morning glory and ginger lilies. Whitewood is the smallest of the cabbage trees and looks quite closely related to cow parsley to me. It never exceeds three metres in height.

Something else I have found out today is that one area of the island has changed its name. That could cause some fun I think.

What was originally called the Wild Cattle Pound is now titled Fitzstevens Estate. It does sound more refined but right alongside it there is still Wild Ram Spring. The area generally is Man and Horse.

15 April

It was only today, within a week of catching the RMS away from the island, that I found that there is a natural pool very close to Sebastopol. I also found an old disused swimming pool near to Teutonic Hall. These finds set the mind working along the lines of where else water might be found, and other than numerous unnamed waterfalls all around the island I also managed to find nine springs. These I have managed to find the names of and they are: Alexander's Spring above Sandy Bay Ridge; Harding's Spring at Cason's forest; Jimmy's Ram Spring near Gough's Ledge; Ladies' Bath Spring near Plantation House; Osborne's Spring near Mount Ross; Powell's Spring at Scotland; Salt Spring near to Briar's Village; Spring Knoll at Scotland; Wild Ram Spring on Man and Horse and there are also some that are unnamed.

I think that all of this proves that quite a lot of water can be around when the weather is right for it. With the very hot weather persisting and a drought seemingly imminent, it seems to be a case of the sooner the better for the island's growers and gardeners. As I have said before, climatic variations are probably nowhere more noticeable than here, with surplus and scarcity finely balanced. At this very moment onions are almost non-existent, yet all around is a luxuriant growth of flowers.

Still with the subject of springs in mind, there is also the side of High Knoll which shows a virtue of its path being traceable by the line through the eroded hillside.

On another theme altogether, something else I did not expect to find was a concrete cricket pitch – laid by the army in West Lodge. My informant tells me another one is on Deadwood, where back in the nineteenth century there was also a racetrack, opened in 1816, where horse racing continued for about sixty years. There is no trace of it now.

16 April

Yet another very hot day. The RMS sailed from St Helena to Ascension Island today.

At 9 a.m. I was at the round-up of the cattle into the pound opposite the St Helena and the Cross church and after that was over, I went on to Cason's and then to Cabbage Tree Road and Hutt's Gate. Between these latter two places I saw as good a specimen of a cock pheasant as I think I have ever seen, flying off with a startled cry as he was unexpectedly disturbed. What with pheasants, chukar partridges and rabbits about there is certainly plenty of game on the island.

Clearing the Hutt's Gate area, the wild ginger lilies and white ladies petticoats are still in profusion, as indeed are the arum lilies now. Wild bilberries are also about in quantities wherever the flax leaves room for them.

Up in the meadows above Black Gate the cattle are now in calf and with the grass being so lush they are looking to be very well and healthy. Moving on and then looking seawards, Bencoolen was standing in all his majesty catching the sun on his different-coloured soils, as indeed were Boxwood and the two Stone Tops. There are so many different hues and shades involved that if an artist captured them correctly on canvas I think the observer would think the artist had overdone it a little. The humped back of Shore Island and the 'perforated' image of George Island stand just out to sea, completing a most satisfying panorama.

Later I saw a video camera recording of the same area, but from a totally different area – the Sandy Bay side from the back of the Two Tops near to the Elephant Rock. That was really good and made me wish I had been there myself. There will not be time this time around, but who knows...

Next time perhaps.

The whole of the Taglate Valley and its continuation Shark's Valley is very picturesque.

17 April

I spent quite a while this morning studying the immigration policy pamphlet that is obtainable on request from the police department. Should any reader be interested I would suggest you obtain a copy of this, but generally speaking the most telling part of it reads: 'all other persons who 1. engage in any trade, business, profession or other gainful occupation; 2. are gainfully employed; or 3. are engaged gainfully as an agent must obtain a work permit. A work permit will only be granted when Executive Council is satisfied that there is no suitable islander available to do the work.' I would think that this is very correct.

For those who do not require to be in 'gainful occupation' then one of four definitions must be fulfilled. They are: 1. Home owners who are defined as persons resident on St Helena who have personally owned a home in St Helena for a continuous period of at least three years. 2. Investors who are defined as persons resident on St Helena who have made a significant financial investment in the island. 3. Persons resident on St Helena who have made a significant contribution to the island. 4. Persons who can show a close connection to St Helena by reason of descent, kinship, residence or interest. This latter qualification could lead to a permanent residence permit being granted but will not entitle the permit holder to engage in any trade, business, profession or other gainful occupation, to take up gainful employment or to be engaged gainfully as an agent. He must obtain a work permit if he wishes to be so engaged or employed.

Again all of this makes good sense, and there appears to be just enough scope for common sense to be used when required.

Leaving the subject of immigration to one side, something that I have ascertained is how Newfoundland got its name. Apparently, way back in 1868, efforts were made to cultivate cinchona – the bark produces quinine – and the name was given to the area cleared for that purpose. In difficult terrain the experiment could never really be a stunning success and it was abandoned when the next governor took over. The name Newfoundland has not been abandoned and is still shown on the maps of the island. Cinchona trees are still growing in the area, but obviously not as marketable proposition.

18 April

Looking at my map today to check on the distance in miles from Pine Gate to Sandy Bay Barn, it suddenly dawned on me just what a large number of places on this island are named simply by colours. With only forty-seven square miles here, I have already found thirty two and I would not be at all surprised if there are even more. The ones I have found, together with their localities are as follows:

Black Gate – between Hutt's Gate and Silver Hill
Black Horse Island – off Sandy Bay
Black Point – off Turk's Cap
Black Rock Island – off Sandy Bay
Blue Hill Village – alongside West Lodge and Barren Ground
Blue Point – beyond Distant Cottage and the Devil's Cap
Bluemen's Field – on Crack Plain
Brown's Hill – near the Dungeon
Chestnut – between Fairyland flax mill and Mount Vessey
Goldmine Gate – near Iron Pot
Green Hill – picnic area above Sandy Bay and Pine Gate
Green Patch and Lemon Tree Gut – from Wild Ram Hill
Lemon Valley Bay – out from Lemon Valley
Pine Gate – near Sandy Bay
Red Hill – near Bishopsholme
Red Hill – near Levelwood School
Red Sand – from High Hill towards Thompson's Valley Island
Redgate – between Red Hill and Francis Plain (water treatment works)
Redgate – both between Blue Hill Village and Tolly's Ledge
Sandy Bay Barn – village and beach as well as Ridge Island
Silver Hill – near Levelwood
White Gate – near Plantation House
White Hill Point – overlooking Sandy Bay Island
White Point – on Man and Horse

White Rocks – at Gates of Chaos
White Wall – at Half Tree Hollow

The weather is showing no sign of changing here in the Blue Hill area with the sunshine being really hot. It is hard work for people working, but for holidaymakers it is absolutely ideal.

This morning at 3 a.m. the fishing party, together with the donkey set off in total darkness on a two-hour walk along the ridge on Ebony Plain to Thompson's Bay rocks opposite the island. They most certainly had an entertaining morning – in fact they did not get back until 3 p.m. – as they caught over fifty pounds of fish in weight. They had thirteen large jacks, two conger eels, some old wives and an assortment of others.

19 April

Today was again quite hot, so we decided to spend it in and around Jamestown. A walk from the wharf steps was first on the agenda, and having watched the various small boats and yachts riding at anchor on the slightly turbulent sea, we walked through the various customs and container sheds, past the old mortuary – it dates back to about 1787 – and so clear of all these buildings, past the two cannons outside the Jubilee Goldstore, the Honeymoon Seat, the entrance to the swimming pool, another seat beneath the trees and so to the archway bearing the East India coat of arms and on into Grand Parade. Here is the treasury, the police headquarters, the prison and a small side street that leads to the bottom of Jacob's Ladder; and of course St James's church – still minus its spire. Various stones and plaques are about, but these I have already dealt with earlier. There is also the courthouse and the public library. Munden's to the left and Ladder Hill dominate the scene on either side.

We did see some skuas today, a sea bird that has migrated from farther north, but which I had not seen before, they were flying and roosting around Munden's. The municipal gardens are very cool and refreshing even in the warmest of weather, due to the shade generated by the giant trees growing there. These gardens were constructed by soldiers on fatigues in 1792.

The various buildings in Main Street are well documented in other books, so suffice to say that trade and commerce are reasonably well catered for. The market hall and also the Canister are both buildings worthy of comment, as is the hospital. The stream of the James Valley, known as the Run, although walled in and so invisible from most angles, is quite impressive when viewed from the hospital.

At Half Tree Hollow is the old cow path winding up from the valley below and this also is clearly visible from the hospital area in upper Jamestown.

What is now a garage above the public gardens was at one time the Paramount cinema, next door to the museum.

On a personal note, we had several songs dedicated to us on the request radio programme of St Helena, as we go back to England the day but one after tomorrow. We enjoyed that, as it does tend to prove we made a lot of very good friends in our time here.

20 April

Four hours of continuous rain during the early hours. It did not inconvenience us but has proved a blessing to the growers. They really did need it.

With only two days left on this island, we decided to spend some of it simply driving around the parts – or some of them – that we had already visited, just for one last lingering look. We took in Thompson's Wood, Man and Horse with Manami Bay, West Lodge, Cason's, the arboretum, Whitegate, Hutt's Gate, Longwood, Rock Rose, Pine Gate, Sandy Bay, Cabbage Tree Road, Francis Plain and eventually back to Blue Hill. We really did cover a number of nostalgic miles through some of the most flower-bedecked countryside in the whole world. It defies description.

In the evening a party was laid on for us in Levelwood as a sort of going-away present. Everyone really threw themselves into it with a vengeance and we were treated to a marvellous time. I cannot imagine anyone getting any satisfaction at all about leaving St Helena. It must be a lovely place to return to.

21 April

The morning was taken up with the packing of our suitcases ready for taking to the customs shed. They had to be left before 3 p.m. ready for transferring by boat to the RMS which will be leaving tomorrow morning reasonably early, Cardiff-bound via the Gambia and Tenerife. There is most definitely a tinge of sadness in the air. This is the worst day of the whole holiday.

On handing over our cases the police stamped our passports and we then made our way to the Consulate Hotel...

It seemed the only thing left to do. I just couldn't bring myself to have a last drink of the usual beer and instead settled for a non-alcoholic beer instead. In a queer way it seemed more respectful.

On returning to Blue Hill for the last time we were visited by three or four families bearing *bon voyage* cards and some going-away presents and this was accompanied by a lot of telephone calls from friends that we had made, all in the same vein. It was a lovely feeling, but one we could still have done without – and stayed on there instead.

Life will never be the same.

22 April

Embarking

We left for the RMS at about 8.30 a.m. and we had a real multitude to see us off, not just the two of us of course, but it seemed that way as everyone seemed to know everyone else.

The most amusing part of the whole departure from the island from everyone else's point of view must have been at the point where the passengers jump – with the aid of a rope ladder when required – from the steps into the small boat that eventually takes them out to the RMS standing in seventeen fathoms of water, way out in James Bay. The sea was so very rough that it took some time to get the boat into the correct position for this manoeuvre and as each person got into it so it was likely to move either sideways or directly from the steps. When it was my turn a gigantic wave came bearing down on me and I was absolutely saturated. Before I could do anything about it, I was hit by a second one. It certainly gave cause for comment. Having got aboard the RMS, my first task was to completely change my clothing.

Immediately before sailing, all of the passengers were given life-jacket drill. We lifted anchor and set sail just after 11 a.m. Less than two hours out to sea, we saw our first flying fish of the voyage. It was basically a day of getting the feel of the ship again and getting to know one's fellow passengers and by the evening everyone was mixing well, especially the ones who prefer the sun lounge area.

For anyone interested a film was showing in the evening from 9.15 p.m. until 10.45 p.m.

It was 3 a.m. by the time we retired after a very busy and entertaining day.

23 April

Up and about by 7 a.m. and in no time at all we were visited by numerous shoals of flying fish. Then, taking it easy, about 10 a.m. out on the port side I saw a humpback whale. There were no sea birds to be seen, not even a wandering albatross. There was a quoits competition held on the funnel deck at 11 a.m. for the entertainment of anyone interested.

At midday, the officer of the watch announced the previous twenty-four hour figures as latitude 10°30.5' longitude 08°10' west; distance to go to Banjul (once called Bathurst) in the Gambia 1,588 nautical miles, distance travelled from St Helena as 353 nautical miles; sunset to be at 6.30 p.m. and the wind southeast at force five. The nearest land is still St Helena.

The afternoon saw most of the passengers going for a siesta either in their cabins or on the deck. It was quite hot today with both sea and air temperature being identical at 26°C/79°F.

At 7.30 p.m. we all attended the captain's 'punch party' with plenty of drink following, and this was followed by a grand barbecue and then a lot of dancing. We even had a talk on the sky at night by the captain. It had been a really beautiful day.

Of each of the days travelling to St Helena and the first two days of the return journey these two had been the best, especially this particular one.

Keep-fit classes are organised every day and also there is a film every day to keep people occupied if they are so interested.

At 2 a.m. we went to bed after an evening in which we had also put the world to rights – in the nicest possible way.

24 April

Now it is getting quite hot and humid with the temperatures at eight in the morning being 31°C/88°F air temperature and 29°C/84°F sea temperature.

Lots of flying fish about today – as one would expect – and also we actually did see an albatross, which was a bonus. Many activities occurred during the day and evening as is usual, with everyone thoroughly enjoying themselves.

With the sun blazing down throughout the whole day and very little cloud cover, many found it a little too hot and spent some time in the sun lounge taking advantage of the air conditioning. Although a few brave souls did see out several hours on deck, they came off it eventually looking like freshly boiled lobsters.

At midday the various relevant readings were: latitude 05°22' south; longitude 10°16' west; distance still to travel to Banjul 1,231 nautical miles; distance travelled in the last twenty-four hours, 333 nautical miles; sunset to be at 6.42 p.m. and the wind south-west force three; average speed 14.36 knots.

The nearest land was Ascension Island. Eventually got to bed at 2 a.m. and slept the 'sleep of the just'.

25 April

This was the day we crossed the equator. The crossing-the-line ceremony was almost delayed or even cancelled on this stiflingly hot humid day due to the probability of rain, but the threat passed and the proceedings got underway. It was similar to the one coming south and equally enjoyable for all the onlookers, although I'm not so sure about the participants. The ceremony is steeped in history and tradition and can be traced back to the Phoenicians who made sacrifices to the various gods of the seas when passing through the Straits of Gibraltar. It has now been transferred to the equator, and of course no sacrifices are now made. Some of the 'volunteers' may not agree with this statement.

What we thought was a school of dolphins was seen out on the port side at about 11.30 a.m., but it was then decided that they were a school of tuna. There were also the usual large numbers of flying fish about.

During late afternoon the heavens opened and everyone was kept off the outside decks by the ferocity of the storm as it was accompanied by both thunder and lightning.

A casino evening was held in the sun lounge throughout the evening until well after midnight and I found that most enjoyable as I made a useful profit.

The midday readings from the bridge had been: latitude 00°11' south; longitude 12°32' west; distance covered during the previous twenty-four hours 340 nautical miles at an average speed of 14.7 knots. The total distance travelled is 1,028 nautical miles in a total time of 71.9 hours at an overall speed of 14.29 knots. There were still 888 miles to go to Banjul. Sunset was at 18.54 p.m., wind was south-south-east, force three. At this time the nearest land was Liberia. Temperatures of both air and sea were 29°C/84°F.

Today we again saw a lone albatross heaving southwards. Bed was at 2 a.m. – again.

26 April

Most of the morning was spent inside in the sun lounge as the weather was sweltering out on deck with the temperature reading air 27°C/81°F, sea 30°C/86°F.

Rain threatened all day with heavy clouds always showing somewhere about us, but it did not actually occur. Flying fish were few and far between and to date have only seen one other boat – an oil tanker – since leaving James Harbour. We are in the area that is called the doldrums.

A general knowledge quiz was held on a knock-out basis to keep those who wanted to occupied, but by the rules in use only one team was likely to win – and they did so. Still, it whiled away an hour or so and gave a lot of people entertainment.

The evening was used as a competition time for the game of skittles in which about twelve teams of four players entered. For our own part, we did get into the last four, but there were two or three very good individual players out there and as a result just about every person involved had a good evening.

We also saw a video film in the making entitled *In Search of the Emperor's Ghost* relating to St Helena and also the search beneath James Bay for the cargo of the Papanui which sank in flames just before the First World War. It looks like it will be a well sought-after film when finally completed.

The midday figures from the bridge were: latitude 04°56' north; longitude 14°38' west; distance covered during the previous twenty-four hours 332 nautical miles at an average speed of 14.18 knots. There are still 556 miles to go to Banjul.

Sunset was at 7.08 p.m.; wind was nil (doldrums), the nearest land is still Liberia.

Bedtime was 3 a.m. It certainly is a time for late nights as there is so much to do.

27 April

I am told that during last night, either swallows or house martins were resting on the boat itself.

At about 11.15 a.m. – whilst a so-called cricket match was being played on number two hatch – we saw firstly flying fish, then a giant ray on the port side, and then about fifteen minutes later two sharks patrolling out alongside the ship. Sea birds were now beginning to appear as well.

As the cloud cover disintegrated and let in the sunshine more and more life appeared on the surface of the sea until the flying fish appeared to be in larger shoals than they had been at any stage of the voyage up to then. Boats began to appear both to port and starboard and we had soon counted eight of them, three freighters, one oil tanker and four fishing vessels. It was obvious that land was in the offing. The jellyfish known as Portuguese men-of-war were also showing up, firstly in ones and twos but at one time – about 4 p.m. – a whole batch of them appeared alongside the ship. There was also a number of tuna about and then, as a bonus, about 6.30 p.m. a complete school of dolphins appeared skipping about in the wake of the ship. What a day.

The midday readings were: latitude 09°52' west; longitude 16°40' west; distance covered during the previous twenty-four hours was 320 nautical miles at an average speed of 13.33 knots. The total distance travelled now stands at 1,680 nautical miles at an average speed of 14 knots. There are still 236 nautical miles to travel to Banjul. The nearest land is Guinea.

Sunset was 7.20 p.m. Temperatures were air and sea at 25°C/77°F.

Bed was again 2 a.m. Have really got the taste of this sea travel now.

28 April

This was a very interesting day. We were greeted by the squawking of numerous seagulls as we moved into the area of the buoys marking the entrance to the river of the Gambia. The twenty-seven nautical miles from this entrance to Banjul – the capital and point we were heading for – were full of colour and incident, as we saw a large number of boats and ships, ranging from small canoe-type fishing boats right through the range up to large container ships and oil tankers, including the loading and unloading of them. Standing along the ship rails studying the scene after we had docked, it became even more intriguing as we saw a street market appear in front of our very eyes on the dock side. It was probably as colourful a scene as one could ever visualise. Bargains were struck, haggling was at a premium, and everyone appeared to have enjoyed themselves.

Whilst all this was going on, a trade visit was in progress, with all of the Gambian dignitaries coming aboard and meeting with the ship's officers and management, hoping to cement a link between the Gambia and South Africa, which at the moment can be considered almost non existent.

As we pulled out of Banjul at the end of this lively sojourn, we saw a fully grown pelican flying lazily amongst the nearer boats, obviously looking for an easy meal, as he was as near as he could be, in order to be safe as well, to the line fishermen sitting along the jetty who – as well as good fish – were catching quite a lot of some kind of watersnake that was proving to be a nuisance to them. Each tine that they caught one they simply hit it to death with a large stick and then threw it back into the sea.

In conjunction with the trade visit, all passengers on the RMS were treated to a free drinks session to accompany their luncheons. Going up the river to the open sea, evening arrived and the coastline became flooded with twinkling lights from the buildings, roads and lighthouses around.

At 9.15 p.m., we watched a film entitled *Dennis* that caused roars of laughter and then the final walk around the deck for the evening saw us taking in the far-off view of Dakkar. As I said, a very interesting day.

With most of the proceedings having been taken up with coming to the berth and then in docking, no daily readings of longitude, etc. were recorded, as they were inappropriate.

An early night today – 1 a.m.

29 April

Temperatures were much down today, at midday the air and sea temperatures were 20°C/68°F.

We saw two side-whales about 9 a.m. and also quite a number of frigate birds were circling around for quite a while. Some flying fish were seen, but not as many as might have been expected. Probably a dozen or so ships and boats of varying sizes and type passed us during the day.

The relevant midday readings from the bridge were: latitude 17°48' north; longitude 17°43' west; distance travelled from Banjul was 270 nautical miles, with a further 648 to go to Tenerife. The average speed was 15.17 knots. Sunset was 8.33 p.m. The nearest land is Senegal.

The daytime was spent, as most were, sitting out on the deck and watching the sea go by or whatever, but in the evening a pantomime 'Cinderella' was put on by the ship's crew that was highly hilarious and quite brilliant really. This was followed by dancing in the sun lounge and that was also enjoyed by everyone, bringing the day to a pleasing conclusion. Bedtime arrived at 3 a.m.

30 April

A reasonably quiet day with most passengers taking the sun on deck as there are only five full days left before we return to the uncertain weather conditions of the United Kingdom. The only bird that we saw today was one isolated swallow, who kept us company from about 8.30 a.m. until just before midday, and we did not see any flying fish whatsoever. What we did see, though, were plenty of working ships and boats travelling in each direction.

For the entertainment of those who so required it, a film was presented in the main lounge at 10 a.m. entitled *QE2, the Queen of the Seas*. It was both educational and interesting. The evening saw the final of the quiz competition, also in the main lounge, and at 9.15 p.m. a film was shown in the sun lounge entitled *Singles*. There was also a deck tennis competition in progress.

The bridge readings at midday were: latitude 24°05' north; longitude 17°08' west; distance travelled in last twenty-four hours was 380 nautical miles, making a total distance since leaving Banjul of 650 nautical miles. 268 are left to Tenerife. The average speed was 15.83 knots, giving an overall average of 15.55 knots, during 41.8 hours. Sunset was 8.36 p.m. The nearest land is Mauritania. The air temperature was 19°C/66°F, and the sea temperature was 20°C/68°F.

I think it was 3 a.m. before we got to bed, but it could have been even later.

Of interest, a drill was carried out today to find six devices planted by would-be terrorists on the ship.

1 May

This was a lovely warm day which began with us standing on the port side of the sun deck watching the outline of Tenerife appear in the distance and slowly, inexorably, draw nearer. Plenty of sea birds were flying about us but we did notice as we drew closer to the island that there was rather a lot of oil floating on the surface. There appear to be some lovely beaches on Tenerife, but in actual fact all of the sand has been imported from Morocco.

We docked at 8 a.m. and were ashore by 9 a.m., but other than the bars and a couple of kiosks, everything was shut. The reasons were a combination of it being a Sunday and also May Day. Street vendors did appear here and there and did a fair trade with Tenerife-printed T-shirts and the like and we also saw newspapers for the first time since 2 January. I don't think we had missed them very much really.

The ship was due to depart on her last part of the voyage to Cardiff at 3 p.m., but was delayed somewhat with refuelling and taking on fresh supplies.

At midday, the temperatures had been air 19°C/66°F, sea 20°C/68°F, although it had certainly seemed to be more than that. We saw neither mammal nor fish life off Tenerife, except for some small 'tiddlers' in the basin.

In the evening a bingo session was held that we attended and after that we were invited to the staff's quarters for drinks and a social session. That was very enjoyable. That brought us to 2 a.m. and time for bed.

The official figures from the bridge were not broadcast today.

2 May

The weather is getting noticeably cooler and at midday today the air temperature was 18°C/65°F, and the sea temperature was 19°C/66°F.

A few flying fish were around and also we saw five dolphins and one killer whale. The sea is now also getting quite choppy.

The midday readings from the bridge were: latitude 33°14' north; longitude 14°19' west; we had travelled 305 nautical miles in 20.3 hours at an average speed of 15.02 knots. We have still got 1,211 nautical miles to travel to Cardiff. Sunset was 8.42 p.m.

One thing that you will have noticed throughout this book is that I have not dwelt on 'the little corporal' – Napoleon. This is because it is almost five hundred years since St Helena was discovered and he only spent six of them on the island. So many reference books have been published relating to those six years that I consider the subject very well covered, to say the least.

Later on in the day we did see several sea birds as we passed within a reasonable distance of both Madeira and Porto Santo. There were also several working boats and ships about.

A couple of films were put on for any passengers who wanted to see them and there was also a talk on the St Helena Association, which is a charity run on behalf of the islanders.

3 May

Temperature is still dropping. At midday it read air 15°C/59°F; sea 17°C/63°F. The sea is also getting quite choppy.

We saw neither birds nor fishes today, although we did see what we assumed to be a sperm whale at about 11.30 a.m. Several passengers were confined to their cabin with colds and I did not escape scot-free either. This type of cold causes a shortage of breath which is not funny on rough seas.

At midday, with the nearest land being Lisbon in Portugal, the bridge readings were: latitude 38°53' north; longitude 12°09' west; In the past twenty-four hours we had travelled 384 nautical miles at an average speed of 14.75 knots, meaning we had totalled 659 nautical miles in 44.3 hours since leaving Tenerife at an overall average speed of 14.83 knots. There are still 867 nautical miles to go to Cardiff. Sunset was 8.42 p.m., wind was north-north-east force six.

For anyone interested, weather forecast areas and surface analysis charts are daily displayed in the sun lounge.

Travel video films were shown on Tristan Da Cunha and also on the seabed of parts of the Atlantic Ocean. For those who wanted more entertainment there was an evening of classical music and over and above to that a horse-racing evening so that people could have a little flutter if they so wished. There is certainly a full programme of entertainment aboard the RMS *St Helena*.

4 May

Until today, every day at sea has seen quite a number of characters 'taking the air' around the deck from 7 a.m. until about 9 a.m., but this morning I saw only four of them doing this and they were – to say the least – well wrapped up against the cold wind that was accompanying the very choppy seas as we passed Cape Finisterre into the notorious Bay of Biscay at about 7 a.m. It begged the question, 'Why did we ever leave St Helena?'

The relevant temperatures at noon were air 15°C/59°F; sea 17°F; and the other figures were latitude 44°06' north; longitude 09°39' west; distance travelled in last twenty-four hours was 334 nautical miles at an average speed of 13.92 knots, giving a total distance of 993 nautical miles since leaving Tenerife at an overall rate of 14.54 knots in 68.3 hours. 523 nautical miles left in order to reach Cardiff. Sunset was 8.42 p.m.; wind north-north-east, force three. Nearest land is northern Spain.

Again, as always, there was plenty of entertainment on the ship for those who wanted it. My own choice was a bingo session, then taking up a joint invitation to an officer's cabin for drinks in which all the passengers at our dining room table attended, and then an hour or so listening to 'Sixties tapes'. This was followed by disco dancing, which certainly caused plenty of laughter whenever the ship pitched and lurched drunkenly.

There were no birds or fish to be seen today, although we did see a fair number of working boats and one container ship.

5 May

Lots of sea birds about today, but fog and mist were both very thick as we entered the English Channel. Several ghostly looking ships, some sounding their eerie sounding sirens passed us throughout the day.

The midday readings from the bridge were: latitude 49°19' north; longitude 06°11' west. We had travelled 344 nautical miles in twenty-four hours at 14.33 knots, giving a total distance since leaving Tenerife of 1,337 nautical miles in 92.3 hours at an average overall speed of 14.49 knots; there are just 180 nautical miles left to go to Cardiff. Land's End was the nearest land and we actually passed that at 4 p.m. The temperatures were air 15°C/59°F, and sea 17°C/63°F.

Rain fell rather heavily from 4.30 p.m. and most of the passengers availed themselves of the possibility of watching the ITV Channel 4, which the ship was now able to pick up, whilst others played bingo or sat talking. No one at all was now on deck which was understandable.

By 7 p.m. the air temperature was down to 14°C/57°F.

We had to pack our large cases – well, any other than hand luggage – and leave them outside our cabins at 7.30 p.m. It did help to take our minds off the 'shortness' of the night ahead. We went to bed a good two hours later than we had meant to.

6 May

The RMS St Helena docked in Cardiff at 3.30 a.m., but no one came ashore from her until approximately 9 a.m., due to the various activities performed by HM customs officers. This did give us ample time to freshen up and dress and also eat a good healthy breakfast of bacon, sausage and two fried eggs, which stood everyone in good stead for their various journeys home.

One sight that impressed me was of a cormorant sitting stock still waiting on a capstan for a fish to appear within striking distance to provide its breakfast.

The 'customs run' was successfully negotiated by 10 a.m., and then it was into the car and away.

A magnificent holiday had come to an inevitable end.